AMPLIFY YOUR MEDIA PRESENCE,

AMPLIFY YOUR BRAND

Dr. Gilda Carle

DR. GILDA CARLE

Amplify Your Media Presence, Amplify Your Brand

Published by InterChange Communications Training, Inc.
Scottsdale, Arizona

Copyright © 2021 InterChange Communications Training, Inc.

Gilda-Gram® is a registered trademark owned by InterChange Communications Training, Inc.

Disclaimer: Private individuals depicted throughout this book are composites. To protect privacy interests, all names and identifying details have been changed, and materials have been adapted or paraphrased.

All rights reserved under international and Pan-American Copyright Conventions. No part of this publication may be reproduced, stored in a retrieval system or transmitted, in any form or by any means, electronic, mechanical, photocopying, recording or otherwise, without the prior permission of the copyright holder.

ISBN: 978-1-881829-25-6 (paperback)
eISBN: 978-1-881829-26-3

Printed in the United States

For more information, visit
www.DrGilda.com

ACKNOWLEDGMENTS

Thank you to all who have generously allowed my research into your world. Your gracious sharing has helped shape the contents of this program for all to benefit. May your AMPLIFIED media presence boost your brand, your leadership, and your bottom line.

Please enjoy my Gilda-Grams®, the inspirational takeaways for you to remember and refer. Reach for them when you need additional guidance and direction.

Also, special thanks to my colleague and cheerleader, Dr. Diane Hamilton, for your suggestions, collegial support, and your amazing cover art design. What a talent you are, but especially, what a dear, dear friend!

TESTIMONIALS

Dr. Gilda Carle is an absolute wonder. Whether she is successful by hypnotizing us into believing we are terrific, or she actually teaches us how to be terrific, is a mystery I will never unravel.
J. Richard Goldstein, MD., Former New Jersey State Commissioner of Health

Female Tony Robbins with a doctorate
Bloomberg Financial News

Best Speaker in America, Editor's Choice
Successful Meetings Magazine

Busiest television therapist in the business
The New York Times

Dr. Gilda elevates the self-esteem of everyone from CEOs to street people . . .
  Philadelphia Inquirer

Dr. Gilda's practical advice and vibrant personality endeared her to millions on my TV show. She's the best in the business.
Sally Jessy Raphael

TV's #1 talk-show therapist; hotter than the Sahara; part philosopher and part stand-up comic.
Gannett Newspapers

Howard Stern: Dr. Gilda, I've seen you on TV. You seem to be very bright.
Robin Quivers: And you always give good advice.

Dr. Gilda is our fave know-it-all.
Teen People Magazine

Package your Gilda-Grams® with Sponsors and get them on air. You're a media star!
Clark Smidt, Radio Broadcast Executive

Your empowerment training for Female Veteran SHEroes is paying off. I never felt so strong! I am so very proud of me, but it was because of YOU that I can actually say that.
Lisa Spencer, US Navy Veteran

The Dear Abby of the New Ages
Laura Smith, WABC Radio On Air Host, Cumulus Media

The warmth and sincere concerns from this professor are real and are genuinely appreciated by her students. Far more than communications classes, hers are truly self-improvement workshops. I call Dr. Gilda 'Mother Teresa with lipstick and The Wall Street Journal.'
Wayne Cioffari, Dean, Mercy College Business School, MBA Program

Dear Dr. Gilda,
You'd flash into class with that sassy red hair and I was in awe! Now, out of all my professors, your name is the only one I remember. Why? Look in the mirror and then look behind you. I am one of the many in the wake of a legacy of encouragement and motivation that you have created. I have been blessed to have you as one of the building blocks in my foundation of my successes. Thank you!
Tanya Hargat, Th.D., Small Business Owner

Hi Dr. Gilda,
People talk about you in comparison to Mother Teresa, and I definitely agree. You came into my life for a month, yet you

have given me more love and awareness for myself than most people I have known during my whole life. I busted my butt for many years to change things like racism in the church, drugs and violent abuse, low self-esteem, and other problems of poor people. I suffered for crimes committed by poor Blacks and Hispanics. And I spent most of my life trying to prove that there are good minorities.

Now, with your help, I am able to move on. Thank you for giving me the tools to discover ME and to learn how to sell myself. I am definitely ready to present my 30-second "commercial" to anyone I meet in the future.

I have a deeper understanding of what it takes to be a manager and what the real power of communication is. After all these years, finally, I have become a Capital "I." Dr. Gilda, I love you for showing me how to love me. Thanks Angel.
Frederick D. Fulford Jr.

Hi Dr. Gilda,
My manager asked me to prepare a presentation for the Department Vice President, the Senior Executive Vice President, and the President of the Company. I felt no anxiety, just a desire to show who I am, what I have learned, and what I can do. After my presentation, on his way out, the President stopped by my desk to shake my hand, and compliment me!

Thank you, Dr. Gilda. Without your experience, strength and coaching, I could not have projected my Power Image to these influential people.
Larry Crilley

Dear Dr. Gilda,
Thank you for your private personal coaching! You say I should be "a killer at work and a kitten at love." Yikes! Can't I just be Cinderella? No, I suppose not. Been there on screen, anyway. I will be in touch. What a great service you provide!!
Celebrity Name Withheld

Dear Dr. Gilda,
I am sure you don't remember me, but I could never forget you. You have an overpowering ability to touch the lives of others. Your coaching offered an experience that was meaningful and unforgettable. Thank you!
Keneisha Platt-Mckie

Dear Dr. Gilda,
I felt like I needed an oxygen mask as I started to write Self-Assessment #1, "My Story" from your book, "Don't Bet on the Prince!" Why was it necessary for me to go through so much heartache for so many years? When I had opportunities to change, I backed away, making excuses all the time. Why was it necessary to have everybody's support in order to make positive changes in my own life?

Since last Wednesday, I haven't put your book down. It is the last thing I read before I close my eyes at night. What I am learning is that I and only I must decide what is best for me. In completing the Self-Assessments in your book, I realized that I lost so much of myself. I never wanted to rock the boat, always feeling that others knew what was better for me.

Also, I learned that I never had positive goals. I let people and things around me set a "cap" on what I needed. What a terrible thing to allow others to dominate me! But your last words to me today were, "When the student is ready, the teacher appears." Thank you very much for being my teacher.

God has richly blessed you. Stay healthy and well.
Annie Samson

Dear Dr. Gilda,
Please nurture your great sense of humor. Your vivacious character and bubbly personality are able to illuminate any measure of darkness. What impresses me most is that these traits are so genuine. I deeply appreciate your concern for all of us. You need to tell me how you are able to keep such a tight schedule, and still maintain such a high energy level. You are precious! Keep sweet. We all love you. Thanks for keeping it REAL!
Pauline E. Whyte

Dear Dr. Gilda,
You are the reason I keep pressing on. You are an inspiration, and your books encourage me to know that no matter what the obstacle, as long as I have faith and confidence in myself, I will eventually come out the victor.

If I had a different professor during this time, I would have dropped out of school. But you make it your personal business to keep us going. That is the reason I kept coming to class: it was like the therapy I needed. It was my get-away.

When I write a book about my life, I would like to dedicate it to you, quote your Gilda Grams, refer people to you, and recommend they read your books. I'm serious. You are a great inspiration!
Patricia Wakhu-Parker

Thank you so much, Dr. Gilda. You have forever changed me. **Patricia Reid**

Dear Dr. Gilda,
Before meeting you, I didn't even know I was lost in life. I thought things were going fine, not realizing that "I" (with a Capital) was missing from the equation, because I was so busy handling everyone else's problems.

Your self-assessments and discussions have helped me rediscover myself, set boundaries, and grow. In your book, "Don't Bet on the Prince!," I cried my eyes out completing Assessment #6, "Do I Put Myself First?" I discovered how resistant I was to honoring my own priorities. This was an eye-opener for me.

I refuse to let people take advantage of me anymore. I have an issue exploding right now at work where I've been treated unfairly. Because of you, I am able to stand up for my rights. The old me would have spoken meekly to my boss, and that's as far as it would have gone. No more, though.

You have also helped me in my marriage. I am now aware that I have needs and wants that must come first sometimes. And I communicate them without feeling guilty. For everything, thank you!
Lisa Pegues

Dear Dr. Gilda,
Thank you for providing insight into my misguided parenting. You helped me see the dangers of self-indulgence, and living my life vicariously through my kids. I learned the need to let go. Some things must be experienced by my children themselves.
Gregory Baxter

Dear Dr. Gilda,
Your astute advice helped me end my relationship. I appreciate your insight and support in our private coaching sessions.
Carl Wright

Dear Dr. Gilda,
Because of you, I have now been promoted! Because you taught me to speak up and go for what I want, I projected my abilities and was included in upper management meetings. My organizational skills and take-charge attitude were a few reasons mentioned about why I was given this promotion. I am wiser, and soon to be richer—thanks to you.
Jodi Hauptman

TABLE OF AMPLIFIERS

ACKNOWLEDGMENTS .... **- 3 -**

TESTIMONIALS .... **- 4 -**

FOREWORD .... **- 15 -**

INTRODUCTION .... **- 16 -**

PART 1: A MEDIA STAR IN THE MAKING .... **- 28 -**

<u>Amplifier 1</u>: Warning!
<u>Amplifier 2</u>: 2 Crucial Questions
<u>Amplifier 3</u>: Some of the Skills You'll Develop
<u>Amplifier 4</u>: 3 Seconds to Grab 'em, 5 Seconds to Hold 'em
<u>Amplifier 5</u>: Who Is Dr. Gilda Carle?
<u>Amplifier 6</u>: Public Speaking Inventory
<u>Amplifier 7</u>: Answers & Explanations to Public Speaking Inventory

PART 2: WHO IS LISTENING AND HOW? .... **- 46 -**

<u>Amplifier 9</u>: How Observers Observe
<u>Amplifier 10</u>: Barriers to Every Message
<u>Amplifier 11</u>: Audience Analysis Sheet
<u>Amplifier 12</u>: Part 2--Finale: The Like Likes Like Dynamic

PART 3: WHAT ARE YOU SELLING? .... **- 61 -**

<u>Amplifier 13</u>: Your Brand Strategy
<u>Amplifier 14</u>: What's Unique about Your Brand?
<u>Amplifier 15</u>: Will Your Brand Sustain Loyalty?
<u>Amplifier 16</u>: Two-Part Video Exercise

<u>Amplifier 17</u>: Part 3--Finale: 10 Brand Strategy Questions

PART 4: PROJECT YOUR POWER .... - 74 -

Amplifier 18: Project a Power Image
Amplifier 19: What's Your Attractor Factor?
Amplifier 20: Speaker's Guide
Amplifier 21: Enthusiasm Assessment
Amplifier 22: Part 4--Finale: Your Audience Defines You

PART 5: WHAT'S YOUR PLATFORM? .... - 91 -

Amplifier 23: Television Appearances
Amplifier 24: Radio or Podcast Interviews
Amplifier 25: Digital or Print Quotes
Amplifier 26: Video Conference Calls
Amplifier 27: Part 5--Finale: What's Your Strongest Platform?

PART 6: ORGANIZING YOUR MESSAGE .... - 106 -

Amplifier 28: Introduction to Your Content
Amplifier 29: Thesis
Amplifier 30: Transition
Amplifier 31: Words of Transition
Amplifier 32: Body
Amplifier 33: Incorporating Visual Aids
Amplifier 34: Conclusion to Your Content
Amplifier 35: Part 6--Finale: Good Structure Sustains Audience Engagement

PART 7: APPLYING YOUR MESSAGE .... - 120 -

Amplifier 36: Purposes of Your Presentation
Amplifier 37: Speech Outline
Amplifier 38: Extra Media Secrets
Amplifier 39: Speaker's Guide Checklist
Amplifier 40: Star in Your Own Commercial

Amplifier 41: Part 7--Finale: Prepare for Unusual Happenings

PART 8: OPTIMIZING YOUR MESSAGE .... - 130 -

Amplifier 42: Rehearsing Your Presentation
Amplifier 43: 10 Interview Mistakes—and How to Fix Them
Amplifier 44: Body Language Spoken Here
Amplifier 45: Case Study: Brand Strategy of a Corporate Leader
Amplifier 46: Eye-alogue, Dya-logue, Mono-logue
Amplifier 47: How to Handle a Hostile Audience with Eye-alogue
Amplifier 48: Your Voice of Choice
Amplifier 49: Words That Count
Amplifier 50: Avoid Technical Jargon
Amplifier 51: Part 8--Finale: Know More than Your Pre-Rehearsed Topic

PART 9: FINE TUNING YOUR MESSAGE .... - 190 -

Amplifier 52: Will Your Soundbites Keep Your Audience Awake?
Amplifier 53: Positive Body Language Checklist
Amplifier 54: Empowerment Checklist
Amplifier 55: Non-Verbal Checklist
Amplifier 56: The Power of Rapport
Amplifier 57: Case Study: Brand Strategy of a Politician Who Lost
Amplifier 58: Part 9--Finale: Humor Can Enhance Content

PART 10: GETTING APPLAUSE .... - 211 -

Amplifier 59: Case Study: Brand Strategy of A Politician Who Won

Amplifier 60: 30-Second Social Media Presentation
Amplifier 61: 60-Second Social Media Presentation
Amplifier 62: 3-Minute Media Interview
Amplifier 63: Part 10--Finale: Respect Your Audience's Time
Amplifier 64: End Notes
Amplifier 65: Gilda-Grams® In This Book
Amplifier 66: More of Dr. Gilda's Counsel

CONCLUSION .... **- 230 -**
REFERENCES .... **- 231 -**

FOREWORD

The role of a media coach is to make you feel safe to go inside yourself and access your hidden strengths and talents. After reviewing and rehearsing the information in this program, you will be safely armed with knowledge and skill to alleviate the usual fears and insecurities of presenting your ideas in public. I look forward to hearing about your successes.
Dr. Gilda

INTRODUCTION

YOUR MEDIA PRESENCE— YOUR CAREER'S MOST VITAL SKILL

Gilda-Gram®
Use the power you have,
or lose the power you had.

After achieving a Master's degree in architecture, and learning the trade by working for accomplished architects, Peter decided to open his own design firm. To grow his brand, he knew he needed to rub elbows with the leaders in his community, but like many proficient professionals, Peter disliked public speaking. He knew he had a problem, and he hired me to coach him. In our first exchange, he described himself as "hopeless." I assured him that over the years I've been coaching speakers, I never met anyone I deemed "hopeless."

At this time in history, our world was going into shock with a pandemic. There was so much chaos, the Merriam-Webster dictionary chose the word "pandemic" for its 2020 word of the year. On March 11, 2020, searches for the word were 115,806% higher than on the same date the year before. Like others on the planet, my sessions with Peter had to be re-configured online.

The man was an attractive 48-year-old who was finalizing a divorce. Divorce is never a happy time for anyone. I asked him assorted questions about himself to determine his feelings and fears. Feelings and fears are at the root of our interactions. As his trust in me increased, Peter revealed that he felt like a failure as a husband and father, and he no one would love him again. The thing about attractiveness is that if you don't feel attractive, you won't project as attractive, and your brand, even if it's you alone, won't be attractive to your audience.

Did this man's personal life have anything to do with growing his public persona? No, not on face value. But yes, it mattered to the total outcome. As a Relationship Strategist and Media Coach, I know that how we navigate our relationship with *ourselves* determines our relationships with others. In circular fashion, others reflect back to us our opinion of ourselves. These others can be in our personal life or in our professional audience. But if we're alive, we're dealing with at least one personal challenge, and most of us have more.

Peter divulged that he feared that once viewers saw his flaws, his new business would crash. When someone tells me he's nervous about speaking in public, he's usually too self-involved. As I switch a client's concentration to the *audience's* needs, his self-critic vanishes!

Speakers worry that viewers will be turned off by their looks, speaking ability, clothes, and even their perspiration. But no one can afford the luxury of such wasted apprehension! Audiences are less concerned about a speaker than they are about themselves. Listeners and viewers are concerned about one thing only: Is this speaker giving me valuable information I didn't have earlier?

Recognize that you have been asked to speak because you possess information your viewers don't. Your persona need not play a starring role. It is your BRAND that is on center stage. Of course, YOU may be your brand, and that's fine, too, since speaking requires you to sell yourself and everything attached to you. But your goal is to inoculate your audience with such positive brand feelings, they buy or buy into your positivity. So, it's never about you. It's *more* about your brand. But it's *most* about your audience's *perception* of your brand—which is *your* job to explain and "sell." So, you are the crucial conduit of your brand's benefits. Perfect? No. Real? Oh, YES!

I guided Peter to alter his focus, we analyzed his past presentations, and we strategized our interaction with his most comfortable body language, vocal intonations, and buzzwords for his different audiences. After weeks of intensive work, he was soon feeling confident. At the very start of the new year, I was a proud guest at his second wedding—on Zoom. If not for the emotional depth of our sessions, Peter would probably not have been ready for love so soon after divorce. As I write this, I smile with pride. Minus the wedding, the same can happen for you!

My role as media coach is to integrate and optimize professional and personal selves, as speakers convey their great feelings about their brand. Feelings do count in today's workforce, because they're honest expressions of a whole person.

When you're doing this work and you see yourself on camera, you will experience epiphanies that give way to positive expressions and behaviors. When I was the relationship expert on all the daytime talk shows, unruly guests would go home, observe themselves on TV when their show aired, and become embarrassed over what they saw. When they returned for a follow-up show, they were more determined than ever to clean up their dysfunctions.

As painful as it was, seeing themselves at their worst motivated them to take on a new best. You, too, will find that assessing your image on video will speed you to amplify your media presence through life.

Gilda-Gram®
There are no failures,
only lessons in what to do next.

Hollywood Squares, Meet Zoom

It was almost overnight that the 2020 pandemic mandated face-to-face gatherings from home locales. White collar workers suddenly transformed into daytime pajama-bottom wearers with business attire on top. That's when participants became stunned to find that very little can be concealed when they were eyeball-to-eyeball. Video calling companies like Zoom and its competitors, Microsoft Teams, Go to Meeting, Google Hangouts, Team Viewer, Skype, and others were widely used. I called it "Hollywood Squares," reminiscent of the 1960s TV game show that had celebrities responding from tic-tac-toe-type boxes.

Years later, "Who's Zoomin' Who?" was a 1985 song performed by singer Aretha Franklin, but nobody could have imagined it would become the tag line for interaction during this pandemic period. Covid-19 changed life as the world had known it, and everything old had truly become new again!

"The illiterate of the 21st century will not be those who cannot read and write, but those who cannot learn, unlearn, and relearn."
-- Alvin Toffler, Author, Futurist, Businessman

Without warning or preparedness, the video call wave turned casual "by-the-way" 3-minute hallway exchanges into formal 30-minute group sessions, with the addition of ready hair and makeup. When the trend began, most employees didn't have workspaces at home. Now the sounds of kids arguing, dogs barking, and relatives barging in suddenly became the new normal. Such interruptions challenged employees to leave good impressions on bosses and colleagues. Complaints of having to shave, dress up, and make up *to stay home* peppered grumblings amid digital unwellness and fatigue. But if business was to continue, these online platforms were the only technology we knew.

During these tough times, I was coaching my clients to quit concentrating on their *problems*, and to substitute focusing on their *power*. For many, we needed to continuously review their forgotten power sources and strategize how to best apply them.

Internet interactions rid the fluff from once-large, long-winded diatribes. While fluff may seem like a time-waster to most, it does provide workers with needed buffers and breathers. These slight "recesses" employees once enjoyed had vanished. Larger-than-life arm gestures had to be stifled to accommodate small computer screens, and employees were seated for long stretches of prolonged inactivity, fearful of the dangerous health consequences.

Soon everyone learned that no matter how long they appeared on these calls, they still needed to follow guidelines to maintain continued engagement. Yet, no one had ever been taught the essentials of presenting in this way.

Gilda-Gram®
**The shorter your time,
the more challenging your task.**

Robert Half Research found that a whopping 76% of 1000 professionals had to participate in virtual meetings as part of their job. Most workers reported spending 1/3 of their workday on camera! These employees never wanted a television career, never felt they needed to perfect their public presentations, and never thought to focus on their eye contact, body language, voice, or buzzwords in addition to their regular content. But practically overnight, a silent edict had befallen every employee:

<u>Gilda-Gram®</u>
If you want to succeed,
amplify your media presence.

Before the pandemic, a 2020 Gallup Poll found that employee engagement was at a low 31%, costing companies a whopping $500 billion each year. A huge portion of the workforce had been hanging out in an unknown space between their assigned jobs and "Who cares?"

But now things were different. Employees juggled cumbersome job descriptions that had earlier been ignored. At the same time, they were trying to sharpen their talents to avoid the warning from Gartner, the world's leading research and advisory company, that their current skills would soon be obsolete. As though the health consequences from Covid-19 had not been traumatic enough!

For employees who had been disengaged, the party was over. Employees' "work muscles" had gone flabby from years of apathy. Playing catch-up on their abandoned skills would be unbearable.

People were now suffering not only from exhaustion, but also from guilt about not doing enough! Introverts felt trespassed on by family AND colleagues, while extroverts were unable to pursue the connectivity that fed their social thirsts. Moreover, the National Bureau of Economic Research reported that 3 million people in 16 locked down cities were working almost an hour more than usual each day. Could life get any more crushing?

By November 2020, Robert Half found that nearly 4 in 10 workers suffered from a new syndrome called "Video Call Fatigue." Always having to be "on" was anxiety-inducing.

Unless someone was wildly egocentric, to also have to stare at themselves on camera for hours exacerbated even the mildest insecurities. One employee on LinkedIn complained of having to attend 7 video calls each day. Others reported using as many as 9 collaboration and chat apps a day.

Many organizations never set clear guidelines for video meetings, because they didn't know how or what to do. Moreover, the rules continued to change. Every meeting, online or offline, needed to include an introduction, a body, and a conclusion with a wrap-up. But instead of structuring quality calls, companies overcompensated with too many calls. Gallup found that only 34% of Americans assessed their mental health as excellent, a 20-year low, down from 43% in 2019. For companies trying to sustain their business, there was no time to even discuss stress management.

Video Call Fatigue also plagued corporate leaders. A vice president declared it was difficult to keep viewers motivated online. On LinkedIn, an executive lamented, "With these video calls, there's not a moment I don't have anxiety. Forget Covid-19; I have Zoom-19."

To add to the anxiety of working from home, The New York Times asked, "Is Remote Work Making Us Paranoid?" Jessica Grose detailed how participants on Zoom calls were obsessing that peers were judging their homes and furnishings. A Twitter account even popped up called Room Rater, where hundreds of thousands of people were rating colleagues' video call backgrounds! With only their own four walls to look at during down time, employees missed the impromptu hall chats to reality-check their paranoia, so they began to participate in such silly ratings.

A new kind of Zoom etiquette came into question as employees participated on their video calls. A school trustee was pressured to resign after being viewed smoking, sipping wine, and falling asleep on camera on Zoom in his own home. Attorneys defended his right to do anything he wants in his domicile. Usual office standards began to fray as people became sloppier while dressing down. Jeffrey Toobin was fired from The New Yorker magazine after pleasuring himself on camera, a California planning commissioner resigned after being caught drunkenly throwing a cat across his living room, and someone reported that 15 minutes each day of his "office time" was wasted by employees showing off their cooing babies.

While in their group settings, it also became obvious when someone was omitted from a meeting. Employees know it's better to be praised than punished, but it's preferable to be punished than to be ignored. Thoughts of those omitted ran to, "Am I getting fired?" One woman found that her paranoia had been right on target: She was laid off as part of a "restructuring," exactly as she read her conference call signals.

There was no relief in sight, even for the holidays. Families chose to gather safely via, you guessed it, the dreaded video calls! An employee griped, "As much as I want to see my tribe, I again have to sit on the same chair in the same living room to communicate with them."

Video Call Fatigue disorder can be understood by Cognitive Load Theory, or CLT: Not only must an employee show up for online meetings, but he must also be certain his computer works, the video call is correctly set up, the lighting looks professional, the WiFi cooperates, the right microphone is used, and his image doesn't freeze during his most impressive statements!

CLT dictates that when the "cognitive load" increases from what a person ordinarily does, his thoughts can no longer be on autopilot. Instead, he is pushed to deliberately prepare every single move, like a neophyte starting out, and continuing to want to make great first impressions.

Add these issues to the homelife demands of meal preparation, children's online learning schedules, rearranged furniture to meet the new necessities, continued changes in government restrictions, health threats, unemployment fears, relationship issues, and operating under one roof with discordant personalities unaccustomed to being cooped up together 24/7.

We know that fatigue of any kind short-circuits information processing, memory capacity, and problem-solving—and it often leads to burnout. By October 2020, LinkedIn's Glint Platform found that employee burnout had reached a two-year high, with no sign of abating. As one woman conceded, "Face it! Now we're all on TV." She was right. Not only were employees "all on TV," but it was becoming apparent that the way they projected their TV presence would determine their incomes and promotions from now

often leads to burnout. By October 2020, LinkedIn's Glint Platform found that employee burnout had reached a two-year high, with no sign of abating. As one woman conceded, "Face it! Now we're all on TV." She was right. Not only were employees "all on TV," but it was becoming apparent that the way they projected their TV presence would determine their incomes and promotions from now on. **Media presence is today's most vital career skill.**

With almost a year of pandemic behaviors behind them, over ¼ of the Robert Half respondents admitted that the novelty of videoconferencing had worn thin. Employees pleaded for a return to phones and emails, the very intrusions they once resented. But with a track record of employee ennui, visual interaction and its accompanying scrutiny were looking like they were here to stay.

Recently, some huge companies said they're shutting down their expensive office buildings, because now they see how much less expensive it is for employees to work from home and still be available. Thrive Global estimated that American workers would save between $2500 and $4000 a year by working remotely, and their companies would save $30 billion a day! Those numbers are hard to ignore. Facebook, Twitter, access management company, Okta, and others are already filling positions for chief remote working officers whose tenure will run beyond the pandemic.

Along with an abundance of corporate restructurings, people began to restructure their lives. Business travel was drastically curtailed. The Wall Street Journal reported that the cutback would probably linger for years, and it might be permanent. The impact on airlines was great, compared to 2019 when domestic and international business travelers in the U.S. spent $334.2 billion. Now employers reasoned,

"Why incur the costs of flying people to our location when we can reach them instantaneously with one free click?"

On the employee side, since they were working remotely with no hope of returning to an office, workers began to travel *one way*, away from the expensive cities in which they had lived to be near their jobs. Since they were working from home anyway, now they could choose localities anywhere in the country with more affordable housing — and be sure to make provision for "zoom rooms."

Some experts say this movement was beginning even before the pandemic. I myself had been offered a TV show role after merely being interviewed on Zoom, and this was pre-pandemic. Now, because of the necessary changes in the Covid-19 workplace, remote hiring has become standard, beginning with the once-dreaded phone interchange, and followed by video exchanges, with allowances for flexi-time to accommodate child care and the needs of more vulnerable populations.

Remote hirings make the talent pool much broader and far more competitive, so, more than ever before, **employees** *need* **projection proficiency** for the phone, online, and off line, too, for occasions when employees have in-person meetings and must make that memorable impact in the one-shot time they have.

Get used to these life changes, because the reduced cost factor suggests they are here to stay! President John F. Kennedy said, "Change is the law of life. And those who look only to the past or present are sure to miss the future."

Those who agonized about spending too much face time began participating in a new audio-only platform, Clubhouse, available to iPhone owners. With only a photo of

each participant, this forum alleviated the need for dress codes, furniture scrutiny, hair and makeup readiness, lighting, and all the other intricacies of being in each other's faces. However, the world is 3/4 Android compared with ¼ iPhone, so it's anyone's guess as to the long-term future of this new platform. For those suffering from Video Call Fatigue, however, Clubhouse sprung into place as a welcome freedom from the rigors of needing to always be physically and emotionally on display.

Media Star in the Making, you've read this far because you want to amplify your projection power. You also understand the rewards your Power Image will bring.

You are never given a dream without also being given the power to make it true.
--Richard Bach, author

So it's Lights! Camera!! ACTION!!! Come in. The doctor is ready to see you now!

Your Relationship & Media Strategist,
Dr. Gilda

PART 1
A MEDIA STAR IN THE MAKING

AMPLIFIER 1

WARNING!

You have <u>3</u> Seconds* to grab your audience.

You have <u>5</u> Seconds** to hold their attention.

*How you use these seconds
will determine your brand's success.*

*Kat Coroy, International Brand Designer, U.K.
**Amy Balliett, CEO, Killer Visual Strategies, U.S.

AMPLIFIER 2

2 CRUCIAL QUESTIONS

Before you continue reading,
answer these 2 questions:

1. **I want to be known for expertise in:**

2. **I want to be known for solving this problem:**

AMPLIFIER 3

SOME SKILLS YOU'LL DEVELOP

- Optimize your 5 Seconds
- Underscore your uniqueness
- Script your "What's In It For Me?" Message
- Project your Power Image
- Sell your brand
- Shine your virtual best
- Sharpen your Attractor Factor
- Seduce your difficult audience
- Communicate your empowered self
- Impress as you Address
- Add value to your Audience
- Grab the "WOW!" Response
- Be Remembered and Referred
- Reflect your audience's needs
- Star in your own commercial
- Leave your audience hungry for MORE

AMPLIFIER 4

3 SECONDS TO GRAB 'EM, 5 SECONDS TO HOLD 'EM

It doesn't matter what you say. It's how your audience hears it that counts. In "The Gambler," Kenny Rogers sings, *I've made a life, Out of readin' people's faces, Knowin' what the cards were, By the way they held their eyes . . .* To know what to say and when, you've got to assess the people with whom you're communicating. Finding mutual interests will grab them, so you're both able to exchange information in the same tongue.

The Book of Lists describes public speaking as more frightening than death! People are terrified of an audience focusing on them, seeing them sweat, or blush, or stumble. And they're especially uncomfortable with people looking in their eyes and reading them, Kenny Rogers style.

Of course, whenever you are doing anything without a script, you might sweat, blush, and stumble — but these aspects of real life gloriously prove you're alive and genuine. Imperfections in Persian rugs make them more endearing, just as cracks in the wall give it character. Celebrate your uniqueness, imperfections, and cracks!

Gilda-Gram®
Do something every day that makes you feel uncomfortable.

It may seem surprising, but your public speaking is never about you. It's about assessing your audience before you even meet them, and adjusting your message to fit their hunger. While he wasn't a sociologist or a psychic, Kenny Rogers was a soothsayer who rightly advised us to read people's faces to know how to win!

If you're feeling self-conscious, get over your air-brushed ideals. As an expert in relationships and the media, I know that audiences engage best with people who are raw and real. "Reality" TV first grabbed the airspace of highly scripted soap operas because there was a public cry for this authenticity. Very soon, reality programming occupied a large sector of the viewing landscape.

Although it's become Botoxed, polished, and highly edited, reality TV was originally set up to reflect unscripted lives, while also peeping into the private lives of others. So, when you're in front of any audience, what difference does it make if you naturally sweat, blush, and stumble? Laugh at yourself when you do! Your audience will feel for you, laugh with you, and cry for you *if* you've hooked their attention by showing them you have *their* interests in mind.

But there's another challenge. The world is overflowing with beautiful bells and whistles in a multitude of formats. Your job as a presenter is to break through all that noise. How?

Gilda-Gram®
No one pays attention without knowing "What's In It For Me?"

Everyone wants a payoff for their time (and money) spent. Whether you're speaking to a live audience, one reporter on the phone, your team, Social Media fans, or Hollywood Squares, we are besieged with some 3,000 to 5,000 marketing messages every day. These messages compete with others to grab audience eyeballs. You may be introverted and spooked by others' impressions of you, or ebullient, forever ready to rumble. No matter what your personality, you still must cut through the clutter of competing communications. So, like it or not, you must be visually out there with a message that is unique and memorable, but that also meets the specific needs of your audience.

Amy Balliett, CEO of Killer Visual Strategies, says that visual communication gets to our brain 60,000 times faster than any form of communication. Further, successful visual content includes 50% narrative, so it's not all about those fabulous visuals. As you will learn in this program, your words are upstaged by your body language and vocal intonation. Your body language is your unique visual message.

Yet, you may memorize a speech consisting of words. When you get stuck on one of these memorized words, and you publicly stumble, it increases your fear, shyness, and feelings of discomfort. Don't fret. With this program, you will learn how to avoid those emotional traps.

For years, many of us were taught that audience attention span lasted a mere 7 seconds. Amy Balliett had thought it was 8 seconds. She researched studies conducted on bounce rate, eye tracking, content sharing, and content engagement by Google, Vimeo, Facebook, HubSpot, and Microsoft. All these companies concurred that audience attention has officially dropped to a paltry 5 seconds!

Amplify Your Media Presence, Amplify Your Brand ignites you to command control of your audience's impatience. You will sell yourself and your information by projecting your unique Power Image. Selling is so important because an audience doesn't know what they've been missing until

YOU enlighten them!

We are all salesmen: We sell someone on marrying us, paying us, loving us, listening to us.
--Garrett Gunderson, chief wealth architect

You will strut your swagger in a way that people will say:

Gilda-Gram®
Time spent with you
adds value to me.

As you apply the same brand behavior as a larger-than-life CEO, you'll notice the difference in your bottom line.

Online presence is more vital today than it has ever been. During our worldwide pandemic, traditionally live speeches and performances were converted to online productions. Today, people are interviewed online for prospective jobs and TV interviews. Sure, live events electrify us with exciting energy. But because businesses enjoy such a dramatic reduction in costs when they replace live events with online platforms, many companies will continue interacting at a distance.

Twitter says its 5,000 employees can work remotely "forever." Facebook expects half its workforce to be working from home in a few years. Gartner found that 80% of corporate leaders plan to have their staff work remotely part-time, at least.

So, unless you intend to live under a rock, there is no way to avoid perfecting your digital image as much as you sharpen your in-person persona. It's obvious that online presence is vital in today's workplace. But for those few times you will eventually be in front of your colleagues, you will have to make those times impactful.

Because of their brevity, media interviews are considered specialized exchanges. They require a combination of sharp and deliberate communications skills, avoidance techniques, and deliverance of your message as you want it to be perceived. On TV, in a mere 3 to 5 minute segment, a person must promote herself, her product, her company, and her story, while not seeming "promotional." That paltry amount of time might also include an interviewer's rambling questions, hostile innuendos, or ancillary conversation. There is no time for warm-ups.

Listeners travel up and down a listening hierarchy. In this program, you'll recognize which 5 seconds in your presentation are especially significant. You'll learn how to anticipate audience reactions, and you will devise creative ways to hook them again and again and again.

If you have expertise your listeners need, they won't care whether you're live or virtual. You will learn how to hook them immediately, no matter what kind of stage you're on. You will *educate* them, but you will also *entertain* them, so they remain engaged. All in all, your role is to provide audience ***edu-train-ment***, as I've named it.

Immediately and confidently, you will answer the constant audience question, "What's In It for Me?" You will no longer feel you need time to build up your nerve, to become ready to roll, or to seduce listeners to accept you. Instead, you will learn how to elegantly deliver your points in precise soundbites, because you will have studied your viewers in advance.

Business success is explained by tapping into your audience's knowledge and emotions and showing you understand them and can give them something they don't already have. This is the key to recruiting your audience's trust.

You will see proof that you've hit your target when people *act* on this trust — by endorsing you, buying your product, purchasing your book, and/or wanting to see, read, or hear more from you. The best proof of all is when you impact not only those who *need* what you have to offer, but actually *want* it, too!

AMPLIFIER 5

WHO IS DR. GILDA CARLE?
AKA "Dr. Gilda"

Dr. Gilda was named "the soundbite queen" by America's national TV producers. She is the media's Go-to Relationship Strategist. Highly recognizable, she has appeared on TV, radio, and in print for two decades, including on Sally Jessy Raphael, Howard Stern, Dateline, and most other national talk shows on TV and radio.

She has written for corporate newsletters and CEO magazines, and has authored 18 relationship and business books and hundreds of columns. Her books include "Don't Bet on the Prince!" (test question on "Jeopardy" and a required college text), "How to WIN When Your Mate Cheats" (literary award winner from London Book Festival), "Don't Lie on Your Back for a Guy Who Doesn't Have Yours" (featured on National Enquirer's Health Page), and the business book, "One Up Strategies Business Schools Don't Teach."

Among many other publications, she wrote the weekly "30-Second Therapist" column for the Today Show and the "Ask Dr. Gilda" column for Match.com. Successful Meetings Magazine bestowed her with the title "Best Speaker in America." She delivers keynote speeches worldwide.

Also, as President of non-profit Country Cures® at **www.CountryCures.org**, she uniquely applies Country Music to empower Homeless Female Veterans. Why? Because Country Music tells relationship stories, and women's lives revolve around their relationships. She stumbled upon this technique while teaching graduate MBA courses. She found that when she used a particular Country Music song to get a point across, her students grasped the information quickly.

Dr. Gilda holds a Ph.D. from New York University in Educational Leadership, and she has been an educator throughout her career, impacting Fortune 500 leaders and Dr. Gilda holds a Ph.D. from New York University in Educational Leadership, and she has been an educator throughout her career, impacting Fortune 500 leaders and their staffs, celebrities, politicians, actors, authors, college and graduate school students, medical and dental school students, physicians, nurses, high tech executives, and TV viewers worldwide.

She began her teaching career in the crime-ridden South Bronx, New York. She later applied the "street smarts" she learned there to her performance coaching of high-level corporate CEOs. Today, she boasts the title "Professor Emerita" from a New York business school. A partial list of her corporate clients includes IBM, Citibank, U.S. Army, U.S. Army Corps of Engineers, Kraft Foods, The Gartner Group, New York Power Authority, Mobil Oil, Con Edison, Newsweek, N.Y.C. Health & Hospitals Corporation, N.J. Department of Health, Exxon, Downstate Medical School, K-Mart, Pitney Bowes, Public School Systems in Scarsdale, Yonkers, Somers, and New York City, the Internal Revenue Service, and more.

Dr. Gilda appears regularly on international, national, and local TV networks and cable stations, radio shows, and Internet blogs and podcasts. She is also quoted in worldwide newspapers and magazines. She has appeared in movies/documentaries, including as the therapist in HBO's Emmy Award winner, "Telling Nicholas," featured on Oprah. She hosted Fox's "Dr. Gilda" TV show pilot, MTV's

"Love Doc" show, and TV shows on Trinity Broadcasting Network.

In the privacy of her one-on-one online setting, Dr. Gilda coaches people from all walks of life, from heads of countries to international business executives. Celebrities say they prefer seeing her online because the papparazzi can't track their coaching sessions by following them to their next appointment. She is the only Relationship Strategist who counsels personal *and* professional relationships, because she has found that we can't segment these different parts of our lives. Because a public image affects their bottom line, companies often subsidize this essential employee training skill.

The first time she was asked to be a product spokesperson, it was for an infomercial. The production company asked her to write her own script and memorize it for delivery on camera. Never being a memorizer, she wondered whether she could pull this off. She did. As time went on, she became a product spokesperson for such huge companies as Hallmark Cards, Harlequin Books, Sprint, Cottonelle, Galderma Pharmaceuticals, Match.com, and others, introducing and representing these brands in the mainstream and social media.

Today, as Spokesperson/Influencer, she customizes keynote and motivational speeches, and does satellite media tours, video news releases, columns, infomercials, podcasts, advertorials, public service announcements, and media appearances. She is covered in print, radio, and television, network and cable, syndicated and worldwide.

See Dr. Gilda's Promotional Reel here: Partner w/ Dr. Gilda

AMPLIFIER 6

PUBLIC SPEAKING INVENTORY

To assess your knowledge about speaking in public, check TRUE or FALSE to the left of each statement.

TRUE FALSE

___ ___ 1. During a live presentation, don't move around.

___ ___ 2. If you use notes, the audience will think you don't know your content.

___ ___ 3. Distribute handouts AFTER your speech.

___ ___ 4. Your introduction is less important than your body or conclusion.

___ ___ 5. After answering a hostile question, renew eye contact with your questioner.

___ ___ 6. The size of your screen determines the kind of gestures to use.

___ ___ 7. If your message is clear, you need not worry about speech structure.

___ ___ 8. For the audience to remember your points, repeat your main ideas 3 times.

___ ___ 9. Don't rehearse possible audience questions if you know your material.

___ ___ 10. Listeners can retain up to 12 pieces of information.

AMPLIFIER 7

ANSWERS & EXPLANATIONS TO PUBLIC SPEAKING INVENTORY

1. **FALSE**: Movement can help engage the audience, unless it's aimless walking or pacing, which is distracting.

2. **FALSE**: Notes are used effectively to keep your place and to sequentially continue the flow of ideas, as long as they don't distract from your content.

3. **TRUE**: Handouts distributed before your speech ends will distract from you and your speech.

4. **FALSE**: Your introduction needs to grab your audience's attention immediately, letting them know why they should spend their time listening to you.

5. **FALSE**: To look at this person again is to encourage another hostile question.

6. **TRUE**: If you're in front of an audience, you can use larger gestures than when you're doing online media. More reserved gestures can better fit into the smaller frame.

7. **FALSE**: The structure of your presentation sets a framework for your content so it can be easily followed and retained.

8. **TRUE**: For optimal retention, some repetition is necessary and even appreciated. But be sure you don't say the same thing in the same way. Vary your delivery!

9. **FALSE**: You can never be too well-prepared. The way you respond to questions will determine whether you and your content will be trusted. Anticipating various questions will decrease your risk of being surprised.

10. **FALSE**: Research has shown that people retain up to 7 pieces of information at one time. However, it is suggested that people's attention spans have diminished in recent times. So, think about offering just 3 pieces of new information, and you'll have a better chance of getting your content to be remembered.

HOW DID YOU DO?

WHAT DID YOU LEARN MOST FROM THIS?

AMPLIFIER 8

PART 1--FINALE:
S-t-r-e-t-c-h Your Talents

Before you begin to speak publicly, tape yourself in your own home. Choose any topic on which you're conversant. I taped this 2 minute, 20 second segment on my cell phone in my office: "Sexless Marriages are Rampant"--
https://www.youtube.com/watch?v=f6htaeM_pKw

There were no fancy lights and the camera was my cell phone. But I prepared and organized my content before I spoke.

I've been in the public eye for decades, and when I see my playback on the small TV screen, I always find fault with SOMETHING! I've also been on the large screen of movie theatres. The first time I saw my flaws so magnified, I looked away!

The backstory on the videotape above is that I tore both my rotator cuffs at the gym, during my overzealous workouts! Ignoring the injury, I consequently suffered from frozen shoulder on one arm, and I lost muscle mass in both arms. I'm rebuilding them, but it's a slow and painful process. I look at my skinny arms and cringe. But I accept that this is my reality at this time.

Are you tough on yourself when you see your photos and videos? A lot of actors refuse to see their own movies on the big screen. Hey, Media Star in the Making, cracks in the wall let the light in. Let your *natural* light shine. The world wants real!!

1. Did this video keep you engaged? Explain.

2. What will you remember about this segment?

3. What would you have liked to see me change?

4. What would you do differently if you were on screen?

5. I deliberately wore the color red. Why do you think I chose that?

PART 2
WHO IS LISTENING AND HOW?

AMPLIFIER 9

HOW OBSERVERS OBSERVE

- Listening is the nicest gift you can give to someone. It is the most universal way of demonstrating affection. Feeling heard is very close to feeling loved.

- Ex-hostage negotiator and founder of the Listening Institute, Richard Mullender, says listening is the interpretation of key words that convert information into intelligence. He recommends listening on the telephone when possible to make it easier to focus without being distracted by visuals.

- A speaker only has 3 seconds to grab a viewer's attention.

- A speaker can speak at 250 words per minute. An audience can listen at 500 words per minute. (Since audiences listen faster than we can speak, we must use body language for emphasis!)

- The brain processes 400 million bits of information. It remembers only 2000.

- An audience processes only 25% of your message. They remember only 10%

- Audiences take their first mental break after ONLY 5 seconds.

- Listeners can only handle 3 sound bites at one time.

- The average person's mind wanders 47% of the time.

- Most audiences listen *only* for the bottom line.

- On TV, the impact you make consists of:
    55% Body Language
    38% Vocal Tones
     7% Words

- On radio or podcast, the impact you make consists of:
    0% Body Language
    78% Vocal Tones
    22% Words

- There are **4 PHASES OF AUDIENCE REACTION**:
    <u>Ho Hum . . .</u>
    <u>What's In It for Me?</u>
    <u>Show Me Examples!</u>
    <u>So What?</u>

- Even if your audience *seems* to be listening, they constantly travel up and down a **LISTENING HIERARCHY**, because they'd be exhausted if they listened at the critical level throughout your presentation. Remember this progression:

    --<u>Simple Listening</u>: marginal intake of ideas
    --<u>Attentive Listening</u>: careful intake with effort to understand and recall
    --<u>Appreciative Listening</u>: appreciation for your body language, voice, and words
    --<u>Critical Listening</u>: evaluating your real purpose, looking for hidden meanings, separating fact from fiction, full listening with emotion

- Listeners want to know **WIIFM? (What's In It for ME?)**

- Listeners want to find out:
    - --What the **BENEFITS** are for them to listen to you
    - --What **PROBLEMS** you can solve for them

- Listeners are not interested in the FEATURES you offer; instead give them the **BENEFITS** you or your product will provide.

And you were worried about how audiences assess YOU?
You don't even enter into the equation.
It's always about THEM!!!

AMPLIFIER 10

BARRIERS TO EVERY MESSAGE

Penetrate These Roadblocks

1. Listener motives

2. Listener attention

3. Listener needs

4. Listener objections

5. Listener comprehension

6. General knowledge

7. Group membership

8. Individual roles

9. Individual experience

10. Individual expectations

11. Individual intelligence

12. Individual listening ability

13. Individual interest

14. Individual sensations

15. Individual biases

16. Timely considerations

AMPLIFIER 11

AUDIENCE ANALYSIS SHEET

Information to Know Before You Meet Your Listeners

1. Presentation Objective_____

2. Size of Audience_____

3. Audience Demographics_____

4. Group Memberships
   a) Political_____
   b) Community_____
   c) Economic_____
   d) Religious_____
   e) Social_____
   f) Ethnic_____

5. Audience's Knowledge
   a) Of the subject_____
   b) Of the speaker_____

6. Audience's Opinions
   a) Of the subject_____
   b) Of the speaker_____

7. Audience's Needs & Interests
   a) Primary_____
   b) Secondary_____
   c) Momentary_____

8. Audience's Values & Beliefs
   a) Primary_____
   b) Secondary_____

    c) Momentary_____

9. Audience's Knowledge of the Subject_____

10. Audience's Knowledge of YOU_____

11. Audience's Opinion of the Subject_____

12. Audience's Opinion of YOU_____

13. Amount of Time You Have_____

14. Who Presented Before You?_____
    How Was S/He Received?

15. Other Considerations_____

What did you learn about *yourself* from this **Audience Analysis Sheet?**_____

***

A lot of competitive noise exists. But don't let that stop you. We're all unique. "Sheeple" try to take on characteristics of the crowd. Consequently, they blend in and don't get noticed. Instead of looking like, doing like, and sounding like your competition, project your powerful uniqueness. Once you know your audience through this **Audience Analysis Sheet**, you will have the keys to direct your comments to their pain points. Your audience will be magnetized to you because you're addressing their needs. It's that simple!

AMPLIFIER 12

PART 2--FINALE
The Like Likes Like Dynamic

Your audience may hear your words, but are they processing your message? Usually, the answer is NO. The reason is, in part, because of their physiology.

The average speaker can speak at about 250 words per minute, and the average listener can interpret information at about 500 words per minute, your listener will only process about half of what you say! That half may decrease to a quarter when a speaker in front of an audience drops his rate to 125 words per minute to allow for vocal emphasis and body gesturing. In any case, the average American listener only processes 25% of what he hears--and then remembers a mere 10% of that! (What test in the world allows 10% as a passing grade?)

Another question a speaker must address is how her audience listens. People never remain steadily glued to each word we utter. Rather, they tune in and out according to this 4-step hierarchy:

1. <u>simple listening</u> of mere blurbs
2. <u>attentive listening</u> of easy directions
3. <u>appreciative listening</u> incorporating the 5 senses
4. <u>critical listening</u> or total involvement.

Needless to say, we would all like our listeners to be at the critical listening step when we speak. However, that won't happen because they're physiologically unable to attend with that much intensity for that much time.

Further, listeners were programmed to accept only 7 new pieces of information at one time, similar to the number of digits in our telephone number. But with the advent of cell phones, we no longer remember each other's phone numbers, and today, 7 is an unwieldy number of pieces of information to recall. Also, we've been trained to attend for not longer than 30 seconds at a sitting, having been programmed by the length of our media commercials.

Today, that number, too, is probably off, because commercials are shrinking to less than 30 seconds, and consequently, people are becoming used to 15-second formats or less!

Without having this information, speaking could seem daunting. To add to the burden, Americans consider listening as a passive event, something we do as couch potatoes. In contrast to our culture, the Chinese language uses a symbol for listening consisting of 5 different characters: ears, eyes, heart, undivided attention, and YOU. So, the way people listen is a learned technique, depending on the culture.

Gilda-Gram®
**What we learn,
we can also unlearn.**

As communicators, before we decide to project our natural power, we have to determine who is on the receiving end. In general, the philosophy is "Like likes like." People do business with people they like. And people like people *like themselves.*

Gilda-Gram®
Like likes like.

The dichotomy is that if you don't fit in you'll be ostracized. Yet, if you don't stand out, you won't be seen. What is a marketer to do?

I had been called to consult for a conservative high tech company. Upon meeting me, one of the vice presidents unkindly quipped, "With your long nails, my staff may wonder if you can even use a computer." We both laughed. I recognized that my appearance was more glam than tech. And knowing that like likes like, I deliberately dressed in what I considered to be low-key for this interaction. But my idea of low-key was apparently not low-key enough for these techies.

We cannot be all things to all people, or all people to all audiences. Despite the comment the vice president made about my nails, I was confident I'd be able to give this company what they needed. I was right! That was years ago, and my nails have gotten shorter with the current trends. I continue to consult for them today.

There is much to criticize about cloning ourselves with people like ourselves. For one thing, we miss out on interacting amid the richness of diversity. For another, we can lose the creative productivity that our differences provide. Yet, the general cloning of employees does offer a subconscious comfort zone.

Corporate personnel often look the same, talk the same, have similar backgrounds and educations, and even enjoy the same sports. At one company I visited in Boston, everyone looked so similar, I had difficulty telling my clients apart.

This is the **Like Likes Like Dynamic**. I coach interviewees on how to look as though they "fit in" to their surroundings, while also "standing out." We are all salespeople--selling our services, our products, and ultimately ourselves. Inasmuch as it is feasible, initially match your image to that of your buyer. The objective is for him to attend to you long enough to process your message.

A saleswoman selling to clients in a large metropolis altered her appearance from suburban pants and sweaters to urban business suits. Her sales soared. A high-powered salesman mirrored the vocal tones of potential clients on the telephone. His orders increased by 35%. **Like likes like.** It's the same when you're in the media. This is why part of your preparation is to complete your **Audience Analysis Sheet** in as much detail as possible. The better you know who's listening to you and how they are listening, the better you'll be able to respond to their needs.

Gilda-Gram®
**All audiences want to sense
they are seen.**

But there is a catch. Does the **Like Likes Like Dynamic** imply that a speaker must become something he is not? NEVER. Nobody should change his or her appearance and end up feeling like a fraud. This can happen if we accept someone else's exterior design as our own.

To live in a body made over by an image consultant, to dress in a style selected by a personal shopper without your buy-in, or to wear white starched shirts and ties when your personality calls for casual jeans and plaid shirts will curtail your natural behaviors. If you're having a problem fitting in by altering too much of your essence, employ this guideline:

Gilda-Gram®
When in doubt, do without.

We all possess wide-ranging behavioral repertoires. We behave differently with our bosses than we do with our spouses; differently with our children than we do with our subordinates. On video, my clients and I together select the behavioral repertoires that work best for them in each circumstance — and these adaptations change. Those that work in some situations may not work in others. The power we project needs to be situational, *always depending on who is listening and how.*

Adapting your power to that of another requires that a communicator does her homework. Is her audience low-key or high energy? Are they technocrats or bureaucrats? Are they willing participants in the corporate culture or are they rebelling against a hostile takeover? To determine these and other attributes of the listener, a communicator must develop keen assessment skills.

Since we all filter information according to our personal selective perception, I developed the **Audience Analysis Sheet** as a standard my clients use before they meet and greet their listeners. Knowing in advance they will be judged on their clone-ability is the first step. Aligning your skills with the needs felt by listeners is the next. Later in this program, after you complete the **Audience Analysis Sheet**, you'll begin to map your approach to projecting your power.

Dan, an engineer with the Clifton Power and Light Company, stood before the local Kiwanis Club. It was his job this evening to inform the 30-member audience about Clifton's new power lines, soon to be constructed in this community. Until yesterday, Clifton was looked on as a community asset, providing hundreds of jobs and less expensive electricity. However, just one day before Weston's presentation, the local newspaper published a study linking electromagnetic radiation from power lines with cancer. The Clifton Power and Light Company was the enemy. And, for this audience, Dan represented Clifton Power and Light.

Dan and I examined the questions on the **Audience Analysis Sheet**. Within only one day, the responses to the questions he had rehearsed were no longer viable. Guided by the **Audience Analysis Sheet**, we discovered the listeners' values and beliefs had been positive until they thought the company might be responsible for an increase in cancer in their town.

Their knowledge of the correlation between the transmission wires and the possibility of cancer was still unknown. But they did know and like Dan as a member of their community. We were consciously counting on the **Like Likes Like Dynamic** to kick in.

What we did was to apply Dan's natural charisma and believability. He explained to the 30-member audience that the evidence was scientifically inconclusive. Any cause and effect relationship was still unknown. He used the **Like Likes Like Dynamic** by identifying with the audience as a member of the community himself. He told them that he, too, would be concerned about a health and safety problem-- if there were definitive findings.

The **Audience Analysis Sheet** was able to prep Dan for the hostility before him. Listeners respect and respond to speakers who are prepared to deal with issues head on.

I am often asked if matching your power to that of another is a manipulative tool. The answer is unequivocally YES. But "manipulation" is not a dirty word, particularly as we understand how people listen. To get people to listen to the message we are communicating requires quintessential manipulative skill. I prefer to call it "styleflexing," because each audience requires a different style, and we must be adaptable in our efforts to be heard. There is never a point to speaking if no one is listening.

Since the power we project determines the responses others reflect, *we are manipulating only our own performance to get our message heard.* Is that manipulation? Or is it wise strategizing? Whatever you call it, you must still "manipulate"--or "styleflex"--your personal thoughts in *your audience's* words, with *their* frame of reference, for it to be processed.

By responding to the following 3 questions, and then applying the **Like Likes Like Dynamic**, there's a chance that the power we project will not be wasted.

3 Questions to Assess Your Like Likes Like Dynamic

1. Describe your *personal* friends according to:
   - socio-economic background
   - religion
   - race
   - age
   - education
   - political views
   - philosophy of life

2. Describe your *professional* at-work friends according to:
   - socio-economic background
   - religion
   - race
   - age
   - education
   - political views
   - philosophy of life

3. How comfortable are you now with this alleged "manipulation"? If you're fearful that you're "selling out," this approach may not be for you.

Based on what you learned about yourself from your answers, what skills are you now ready to incorporate into your next presentation?

Summary

To get an audience to listen to you, analyze who's listening. Comfortably clone your style to your audience, but ONLY TO A POINT. When *they* are ready to receive your message in *their* language and style, you'll easily be heard! You face your audience to make an impact that will enhance their lives.

PART 3

WHAT ARE YOU SELLING?

AMPLIFIER 13

YOUR BRAND STRATEGY

<u>What is a Brand?</u>
A brand is your audience's *perception and experience* of a product, service, encounter, organization, or person that *distinguishes it from its rivals*.

Seth Godin, author and dot com business entrepreneur explains that people don't buy goods and services. They buy relationships and magic. Marketing is not about the products you make, but about the stories you tell. So, what matters most is the audience's *perception, experience, and emotional connection to your brand*, not the brand itself. Every brand is unique. But someone must SELL its *uniqueness* to the audience. And knowing as much as you do, that salesperson must be you.

<u>A Strong Brand</u>
--assigns consistent identity and personality to an offering
--creates recognition and distinctness
--supports marketing during promotion
--increases value
--insures trust

<u>Your Objective is to motivate people to:</u>
1. **perceive** your brand positively
2. **love** your brand
3. **remember and refer** your brand
4. **open their wallets** for your brand

<u>Audiences buy and buy into brands they:</u>
-- recognize
-- know

-- trust

Branding consultant from India, Aashish Pahwa, names McDonald's as the sixth most important brand in the world, valued at $129 billion. Its big M logo, its red and yellow colors, and its Ronald McDonald mascot are memorable. And McDonald's volume of business proves that consumers consistently recognize, know, and trust the brand Consequently, they flock to experience McDonald's, proving it's not the branding itself that matters, as much as the way the branding makes them FEEL.

After you grab audience attention in **3 seconds**, you get **5 seconds** before your audience's minds drift. A Harvard study found that the mind of the average person wanders 47% of the time, and a wandering mind is an unhappy mind. So, let's consider you've got a mere **8 seconds to make your audience so happy they'll stick with only you while you're speaking.** Audiences are unforgiving in their impatience and their desire to be entertained. If you fail to grab them *at once*, your competition will. No apologies, no hard feelings!

Gilda-Gram®
Your Brand Strategy must be
<u>Remembered</u> and <u>Referred</u>

How?
<u>Answer These 2 Questions:</u>

1. How do I want my brand to be <u>PERCEIVED</u>? (My Goal)
    ... the go-to brand? ...the healthy brand? ...the reliable brand? ...the trustworthy brand? ...Or, ...

2. What <u>EMOTIONS</u> do I want my audience to <u>FEEL</u>?

Emotions are bodily reactions that spark conscious Feelings. The two words are often interchanged, but they are, in fact, two sides of the same coin.

<u>Gilda-Gram®</u>
Emotions and Feelings
motivate buying and buying into.

Psychologist and expert on emotions, Paul Ekman, grouped emotions into 5 categories:

1. **Anger** (annoyance, frustration, bitter, infuriated, irritated, mad, vengeful, insulted)
2. **Fear** (worry, doubt, nervous, anxious, terrified, panicked, horrified, desperate, confused, stressed)
3. **Sadness** (loneliness, heartbroken, gloomy, disappointed, hopeless, grieved, unhappy, lost, troubled, resigned, miserable)
4. **Disgust** (dislike, revulsion, loathing, disapproval, offended, horrified, uncomfortable, nauseated, disturbed, withdrawn, averse)
5. **Enjoyment** (happiness, love, relief, contentment, amusement, joy, pride, excitement, peace, satisfaction, compassion)

Which of these do you want to instill in your audience? How do you intend to achieve that?

<u>Brand Strategy Agenda</u>

What is your Goal?
Which Emotions Reflect It?
Which Images Invoke It?

1. GOAL

_____

2. EMOTIONS

_____

3. IMAGES

_____

1. How long did it take you to complete these 3 questions? Why?

2. What did you learn from completing these questions?

3. What will you do next?

AMPLIFIER 14

WHAT'S UNIQUE ABOUT YOUR BRAND?

The most successful companies build strong emotional bonds with their customers. These customers, in turn, loyally express positive feelings for these companies.

A division of a Fortune 50 bank on Wall Street called me in to devise a solution to their flagging employee engagement. During our initial meeting, after listening intently, I told the group what I was sensing and how I would approach their issue. I promised, "By the time my program is finished, your employees will feel a lot better about themselves." The director shot back, "I don't really care how they feel about themselves." He was so off base that without missing a beat, I smiled using my South Bronx assurance, and replied, "Oh, yes you do."

The meeting ended and I left, with the director stoically mouthing, "Thank you for meeting with us. We'll let you know how we decide to proceed." I figured my assertiveness and confident overstepping would blow my prospects.

But the next day, I received a call from the director's assistant asking me when I could start to customize a program for them. I completed my **Audience Analysis Sheet**, and tailored a 10-week program for them. The **Audience Analysis Sheet** captured this client's pain points.

We promptly saw an improvement in employees' attitudes and motivations, and the Wall Street bank's profits quickly rose. My program was so successful that other divisions in the company asked me to do the same for them. I continued my performance coaching with different Wall Street audiences for years after that. While many of the executives didn't understand how I was able to create what they called my "magic," the bottom line was healthier than it had been before I appeared on the scene.

Yet, it was still hard for me to describe the how's of my customized brand. That is, until the Showtime TV series, "Billions," became so popular. Finally, viewers were able to see performance coach, Dr. Wendy Rhoades, in action. They saw her operate with clients' personal and professional lives, just as I customarily did. Now, when people asked what I did for corporations, I referred them to the pop culture series, with the humorous caveat, "This is what I do, minus the sex and the drama."

Look around you. Are you missing some obvious creative ways to popularize your unique brand?

I enjoy unifying people and concepts thought to be polar opposites. For example, years ago, when I wrote a TV relationship show for teens, I could have enacted the role of the sole show host. But my gut told me to go out on a limb, so I found the very popular pop culture rapper at the time, Coolio, who was touring Europe. I asked him to return to the U.S. to co-host the show with me.

The visuals were wild: black vs. white, rapper vs. professor, flighty vs. grounded. The concept worked, until I pulled the plug because of my manager's abusive behavior. However, my unusual visual concept was revised when Martha Stewart co-hosted what turned into a very popular Food Network show with rapper, Snoop Dog. I believe that if we don't act on a unique idea we have, it will seep into the ethers, and someone else will.

Your objective is to be **Remembered and Referred**. Do you dare to bend your boundaries? You will, if you write them in pencil, and allow for free-flowing alteration when the circumstances require. I write all my calendar entries in pencil, and with its eraser, I easily switch things around during our changing times.

AMPLIFIER 15

WILL YOUR BRAND SUSTAIN LOYALTY?

In the wild era of Instagram influencers, where younger buyers are fickle for what's currently trending, brands have believed they should only focus on marketing to these millennials. In fact, consumers 55+ were already the most loyal brand consumers, so brands felt they didn't have to invest marketing effort in that population. These seniors command 71% of the nation's wealth.

But life changed with the 2020 pandemic. Suddenly, favorite brands were unavailable, and gray-haired consumers had to pivot towards less familiar staples like toilet paper, paper towels, and tissues. Time progressed, and these consumers found they could make do with other brands.

Now, previously favored brands need to confront their fear of marketing older. Until now, seniors and their buying power have been taken for granted. This may not be the case anymore.

Seniors appreciate service, quality, and value—and with large disposable incomes, they're willing and able to spend for these conveniences. Traditional marketing to seniors has comprised pharmaceuticals, incontinence remedies, and geriatric devices. But thanks to the pandemic, seniors have awakened to the buying power they wield. Suddenly, their aged wisdom ponders, "Why should I pay for the advertisements? What has my brand done for me?"

For example, I was a devoted customer of the indestructible printers from Hewlett Packard. That was the only brand I would purchase. When I needed technical assistance, I'd dial their digits and be connected to an English-speaking tech expert who was patient, supportive, and able to help.

But my last experience with HP was awful. I was connected to someone in Asia whose command of English was too limited to decipher my issue. If I wanted more responsive assistance, I was told that I needed to pay a fee. As a result of that interaction, I will never purchase an HP product again. I doubt whether they care about losing me as a consumer, but I have told everyone I know, and their brand is no longer a favorite in my circle. Instead, I switched to Canon whose English-speaking customer service department is available to supply technical help for free.

During the pandemic, in an effort to cater to this powerful purchasing demographic, some supermarkets provided special hours reserved solely for seniors. I recently called a plumber who discounts seniors 10% off their bill. In the battle for seniors' brand loyalty, brands must be in it for the long haul. Because even if advertisements are attractive, senior wisdom can sense empty words without backup, and they will withdraw support for these brands.

In her "Actionable Marketing Newsletter," marketing expert, Heidi Cohen advised that brands today must have higher social purpose than just creating profit. That includes showing consumers you care about them. Community outreach is a must.

AMPLIFIER 16

TWO-PART VIDEO EXERCISE

Make your Brand Relatable

1. <u>Tape a 30-second video *all about your brand.*</u>

How did you feel?

What did you discover?

Caveat: Brand presentations should not reflect your personal agenda. Instead, echo your *audience's needs, interests, and emotions.*

Gilda-Gram®
True relatability replaces
the SELL with the TELL--
and adds FEELINGS.

*Less **pressure** to buy = more **desire** to buy into*

2. <u>Tape a 30-second video *inspiring your audience with your brand.*</u>

Inspiration can create a lasting relationship. Try it now.

  1. How did you feel?

2. What did you discover?

3. What were the differences between your two 30-second presentations?

4. As a result of this exercise, how will you adjust your future presentations?

AMPLIFIER 17

PART 3 FINALE:
10 Brand Strategy Questions

For optimal success,
DO NOT CONTINUE READING
until you answer each of these questions:

1. Who is your **TARGET AUDIENCE**?

2. What are their **PAIN POINTS**?

3. What audience **ACTION** or **TRANSFORMATION** are you seeking?

4. What is your **BRAND MESSAGE**?

5. What is your **OFFER**?

6. How do you plan to **INTERACT** and on which **PLATFORMS**?

7. What is the **POINT OF PURCHASE**?

8. What is your **TIMELINE**?

9. How will you **MEASURE** your progress?

10. How will you **ADJUST YOUR STRATEGY**?

PART 4
PROJECT YOUR POWER

AMPLIFIER 18

PROJECT A POWER IMAGE

Adapted from "Don't Bet on the Prince!," written by this author

"Our deepest fear is not that we are inadequate.
Our deepest fear is that we are powerful beyond measure."
---Marianne Williamson

TASKMASTER'S CHECKLIST

Are you a Taskmaster? Check the items below that apply to you:

1. Do you need to have a hand in everything?
2. Do you hold on to issues?
3. Must you be right?
4. Do you lay blame on others?
5. Are you short-tempered and impatient?
6. Are you a poor listener?

If you checked even one item, you may have some Taskmaster tendencies.

The issues of power and control go hand in hand. The question, however, is how we demonstrate our power, and over whom we wield control. We are most comfortable when we feel we exercise choice over our own circumstances. Those of us who feel we have lost our right to choose our circumstances--whether real or imagined--sense a loss of personal power. When we feel that our power is depleted, we become unbalanced, and attempt to regain equilibrium in whichever way we can.

Overbearing Taskmasters often denigrate other people. Observe the nasty manager, the greedy secretary, the irate office mate, or even the abusive corporate executive as "unempowered." These people attempt to control *their* life by controlling the lives of others.

John clearly tried to dominate his assistant by publicly humiliating him, falsely assuming that his vacuous superiority would impress other employees. Often, however, the Taskmaster ploy backfires. Brow-beating is nothing more than bullying, and power abuses don't always go unchecked. Beaten-down employees seek solace elsewhere, where they can feel appreciated, rather than oppressed.

<u>**Gilda-Gram®**</u>
The Taskmaster who feels out of control often aims to control others.

As much as the Taskmaster may try to control others, the problem is that no grownup or even child does exactly what we want all the time — and most either rebel or leave. So, the Taskmaster whose goal is to control finds himself constantly miserable, *himself out of control*. Sometimes the controlling Taskmaster finds someone else to replace the loss, but not for long. Evolved employees will not withstand oppressive governance over time.

<u>TOASTMASTER'S CHECKLIST</u>

Are you a Toastmaster? Check the items below that apply to you:

1. When something goes wrong, do you blame yourself?

2. When something goes wrong, do you blame yourself?

3. Do you walk on eggshells so as not to upset others?

4. Do you keep your feelings and opinions under wraps?

5. Have you re-created your appearance and behaviors to mirror others?

6. Have you allowed your boss decision-making rights over your life?

7. Do you yield to your boss' demands at the expense of taking care of yourself?

If you checked even one item, you may have some Toastmaster tendencies.

Toastmasters scurry to meet everyone else's demands while ignoring their own needs. This was evident at a seminar I was conducting for nurses, "Caring for Yourself While Caring for Others." The room was filled with tired nurses of all ages, shapes, and sizes. Many were overweight, most requested "smoking breaks," and all admitted to being stressed beyond repair.

As other nurses in the room slouched in exhaustion, Caroline nodded her head with a smirk. She volunteered to address the group with her findings: "OK, I'm guilty." She rose as she continued, "Yes, my goal is to please you. Yes, when hard-pressed, I'll change my opinions to yours. Yes,

I'll put off my own stuff if you call for help. Yes, Yes, Yes. I CARE TOO MUCH AND I'M BURNED OUT!"

She continued, "But I also sit on my car horn in traffic, I'm pissed off when things aren't done to perfection, and I'd rather do everything myself than see them screwed up by someone else. I checked all the items in *both* the Taskmaster and the Toastmaster categories. I'm in a constant state of panic and stress! Heeeeeelp!"

The audience rose and applauded, because they identified with this burned out nurse. Being *both* a Taskmaster and a Toastmaster is common. Extreme behavior in one realm often catapults us toward extreme behavior in the other.

<u>**Gilda-Gram®**</u>
**The Toastmaster who feels without control
often becomes depressed and/or angry
for suppressing his own voice.**

For some, Toastmaster-induced depression and anger are not enough. The most imbalanced might commit workplace violence. And I have seen Toastmaster women bolt from their entire family, including their small children. *Watch the fabulous Carmen raise 3 kids singlehandedly, organize and maintain a home, run a small business out of her basement, oversee the cooking, ironing, and laundry, heal the physical and emotional wounds of everyone under her roof, including the dog who just got into a spat with the cat . . . See her today, for this is her final performance.*

Most bolters view only two alternatives: to leave or to die. This is serious business. Could anyone have predicted a Toastmaster's price of nice? Always predicated on a desperate desire to be liked.

Where does your power lie? Do you lean to the side of too much control? Do you offer too much abdication? Like Nurse Caroline, do you unwittingly swing between the two?

<u>Gilda-Gram®</u>
**When you like yourself, you trust yourself.
When you trust yourself, you voice your feelings.**

If liking yourself involves empowering yourself, and power is too unwieldy a concept, how do you go from Point A to Point B without turning off those with whom you regularly engage? The answer is to avoid the extremes and select the power source you need *at the time*--Task or Toast. To take a stand one way or the other, become equally comfortable with applying both.

Incorporate Balance between Taskmaster & Toastmaster

Being in control is important, but so is giving up the crown to compromise. The positive traits of Taskmasters involve accomplishing quests quickly, competently, methodically. The positive traits of Toastmasters involve their consideration for other's feelings and needs. Neither alone is bad. But one without the other is impossible. Pressing task achievement burns people out as much as happy-making questions their own life's purpose.

The ability to assess circumstances for what they are, and then style-flex the power base best suited to the situation is the true measure of power. Power draws from a feeling that you are empowered enough to compromise. But it never means that you give so much away that you feel you are left with nothing.

DR. GILDA CARLE

Which Runs My Life —
My Internal or My External Power?

For each pair of statements, circle either (a) or (b) that you believe is most true:

1. a) People usually don't realize all I do for them.
   b) I usually get the appreciation I deserve.

2. a) I often have bad luck.
   b) My misfortunes are usually caused by my mistakes.

3. a) Even when I try to win their favor, some people just don't like me.
   b) If someone doesn't like me, it's often because I haven't spent enough time with them.

4. a) It's tough to tell which people have my best interests.
   b) My friendships require my time and energy.

5. a) I usually have little influence over what happens to me.
   b) When I'm lonely, it's usually because I'm not reaching out enough.

Scoring Key
Count the number of a)'s you circled. If you circled only one, you are probably controlled Internally. If you circled 2 or more, you are probably motivated by External forces.

Gilda-Gram®
Power is never control *over*.
Control *over* verifies a person's insecurity.

Real power expresses our deepest sense of inner peace, our comfort in knowing who we are and what we deserve. Knowing what we stand for, and being willing to state it, remains our greatest strength. Our power gives us the pen with which we draw our boundaries. When someone crosses our sacred, private line, our power directs us to boldly hold to "No."

We must use our power to observe our innermost feelings and follow their lead. Our innermost feelings are based in Internal Control. Despite cries from the crowd, Internally-Controlled people remain self-directed without swaying to the noise outside. Inner-oriented personalities pride themselves on their individuality. Marching to the beat of their own drummer finds them happier and healthier. They know who they are, they pursue what they want, and they styleflex between the two power alternatives in accord with their own goals.

The opposite of Internally-motivated people are those driven by External Controls. People influenced by External incentives allow themselves to be directed by the arbitrary dictates of others. In kiss-the-right-ass confusion, Externally-Controlled personalities want to impress, please, and seek acceptance by the in-crowd.

As with the Taskmaster versus the Toastmaster, every healthy person must balance Internal and External Controls. While Internally-Controlled people certainly exhibit more independence and self-awareness, to live *totally* by Internal controls could mean utter self-absorption.

On the other hand, to remain at a job with someone who is abusive or condescending, is an example of buying the External tradition at the expense of the self. As with everything, it is always the measure of degree and the question of excess. The optimal power balance consists of being *guided* by Internal Controls and *motivated* by External Controls.

<u>Gilda-Gram®</u>
**Power is as power does.
Power does as power feels.
Power feels as power thinks.
Think power, project power.**

How To Project A Power Image

When we know our power, we attract people who are comfortable with it and unthreatened by it. We project what I call a *Power Image.*

The concept of Power Image came to me while I was doing consulting for Fortune 500 companies with mostly men. I studied how the most successful among them strutted their power, yet didn't act imperious. Their posture, their pitch, and their pronunciation all subtly connoted they were in charge. I observed their staffs willing to walk through walls for them.

In contrast were the men who repeatedly needed to remind their employees that they were the boss. I noted how their staffs resented and resisted their directives. Clearly, their power was based purely on their legitimate authority as hired guns, not on their genuine likeability and devotion to their employees and goals.

A Power Image begins in our mind, but comes alive through our body language, voice and words. When we think the thoughts we need to think, we become transformed.

My Power Image keynotes often draw standing-room-only crowds. Projecting a Power Image is potent because it doesn't scream, "I am in charge." *It doesn't need to scream.* People just know.

AMPLIFIER 19

WHAT'S YOUR ATTRACTOR FACTOR?

Measure your Power Image by your "Attractor Factor." If you engage your audience well, they will buy your product, alter their mindset, or change their behavior. That's how you know your Attractor Factor is high. Congratulations! If your audience is more ho-hum, you still have work to do.

Create a collage of yourself as you demonstrate a Power Image. How does this collage describe your brand of Attractor Factor? Why?

When your Attractor Factor is high, you will feel it and vibrate it. We always attract people and experiences with vibrations similar to ours. Now the question is, "How can we optimize our positive mutual vibes?" (As I write this, I smile, because it sounds like a topic I'd discuss on the personal side. Note its similarity to the professional side.)

How to Apply Your High Attractor Factor

Leadership Consultant, Karen Eber did a fascinating TEDx talk at Perdue University titled, "How Your Brain Responds to Stories -- and Why They're Crucial for Leaders." She advocates for leaders to tell stories so audiences feel seen.

The technique involves using vivid descriptors that draw feelings to glue your audience to your tale. For example, "the wet leaves fell" could be enhanced by saying, "the heavy, cold leaves, weighted down by the icy rain that blanketed the night, fell loudly to the ground." While the first description is adequate, the second gets listeners to feel the chilly picture, and it is that emotion that bonds speaker to listeners. Great stories build audience tension and bond listeners' attention to the speaker and the scene.

Eber explains that a speaker telling a descriptive story while his listeners visualize his words "neurocouples" brain excitement between listener and speaker. Like a scientific game of dominoes,

1. The listener *experiences* the tension of the story.
2. He feels empathy for the storyteller.
3. Increased empathy increases oxytocin, the feel-good chemical.
4. While listening and experiencing, oxytocin is released into the listener's brain.
5. The more oxytocin the listener has, the more trustworthy he deems the speaker.

All leaders aim to build trust. Storytelling can be the cutting-edge tool for trust-building. Watch Eber's TEDx to see how descriptive storytelling can bring to life even dull corporate data!

How will knowing these storytelling principles change your presentations?

AMPLIFIER 20

SPEAKER'S GUIDE

SPEAKER'S GUIDE

AUDIENCE FOCUS	SPEAKER'S OBJECTIVE	SPEAKER'S APPROACH	SPEAKER'S TECHNIQUE	SPEECH FORMAT
▪ Ho Hum...	▪ Motivate	▪ Engage	▪ Hook Attention	▪ Introduction
▪ What's In It for Me?	▪ Communicate	▪ Encompass ▪ Enlighten	▪ Main Idea #1 --Detail (a) --Detail (b)	▪ Body
▪ For Example!	▪ Illustrate	▪ Enthuse	▪ Examples ▪ Visuals	
▪ So What?	▪ Activate	▪ Enlist	▪ Command Action ▪ Command Reaction	▪ Conclusion

www.DrGilda.com

AMPLIFIER 21

ENTHUSIASM ASSESSMENT

Watch 2 different speakers on 2 different newscasts. Complete this form for each, comparing their performances.

1. **Vocal Delivery**
    a. Low (monotone, poor articulation)

    b. Medium (some variation in pitch, volume, speed)

    c. High (dramatic changes from louder to softer tones)

2. **Eyes**
    a. Low (avoids eye contact; seldom raises brows)

    b. Medium (appears interested; occasionally lights up)

    c. High (active; maintains eye contact without staring)

3. **Gestures**
    a. Low (rigid; seldom moves arms)

    b. Medium (occasionally moves body)

    c. High (demonstrative body, head, arm, hand, face moves)

4. **Body Movement**
    a. Low (seldom moves from one spot)

    b. Medium (occasional movement)

c. High (unpredictable, energetic, natural body movements)_____

5. **Facial Expression**
   a. Low (Deadpan; expressionless; frowning)
   _____

   b. Medium (agreeable; occasional smiling)
   _____

   c. High (vibrant; multi-expressioned)
   _____

6. **Word Selection**
   a. Low (mostly nouns; few descriptive adjectives, simple language)_____
   b. Medium (some adjectives; repetition of the same ones_____
   c. High (highly descriptive variety of language expressions_____

7. **Overall Energy Level**
   a. Low (lethargic; inactive; sluggish; dull)
   _____

   b. Medium (shows even energy)
   _____

   c. High (exuberant; energetic)
   _____

AMPLIFIER 22

PART 4--FINALE
Your Audience Defines You

We've been discussing your need to focus on your audience. The beauty of speaking live is that you get feedback immediately about how you're being received, and you can adjust your delivery accordingly. But when you're speaking live online, your knowledge of your reception is limited to who contacts you later. On the live online portals, keep presenting yourself as often as possible. After a while, you'll be able to assess the interest you get. Or, you can calculate interest by the number of people who purchase your product or book or whatever you're selling.

Video: "Does Friends with Benefits Work?":
https://www.youtube.com/watch?v=gf_tbU5u7AM

<u>Backstory</u>: I rarely have a perfect day on a set—which is what makes each appearance so exciting! At this taping, I had just been getting over laryngitis! In addition, my hair had been professionally done, but I walked out into the humid New York air, and the style frizzed.

To top that off, during the shoot, the cameraman continued complaining that my taffeta blouse was making too much noise each time I became my animated self. My animation is my trademark on television, but this camera guy wasn't having the accompanying racket. Nor was I willing to become a piece of cardboard, demonstrating no emotion. Eventually, we came to a compromise.

Despite setbacks, somehow every show goes on. Because

you're on this journey with me, you're hearing this backstory. *But audiences care only about what they see on screen.*

<u>**Gilda-Gram®**</u>
**Content must be appealing,
and delivery must be compelling.**

Our painful preparation is irrelevant to our viewers.

1. In the short 51 seconds of this video, did you as a listener remain engaged? Why or why not?

2. What will you remember about this segment?

3. What would you have liked to see me change?

4. What would you do differently if you were on screen?

PART 5
WHAT'S YOUR PLATFORM?

AMPLIFIER 23

TELEVISION APPEARANCES

This Amplifier discusses presenting on the TV platform. Next we'll discuss the radio and podcast platform, the digital and print platform, and video conference calls. Whichever platform you are on, you will still need to employee well-structured organization, pre-set discussion points, and animated speaking essentials, all included in this program.

For starters, let's place the term *presentation* aside. Instead, think of having an interesting and/or fun *conversation*, using your natural expressions. I was the Performance Coach for a mid-sized sales company in Manhattan when one of the salesmen came to me distraught. Before being in sales, he had been an actor, a field he had to leave at the height of his success, only because he began to panic and vomit each time he was to appear on stage.

Now, years later, as a very successful salesman, each time he had to address an audience, he once again restarted his nauseous feelings. Like old times. As I began to coach him over his fears, I questioned what he was thinking about when the panic attack started. He said the word "presentation" was daunting, and he worried about how people would assess him.

As soon as I replaced that word with the more acceptable term "conversation," he lit up. I also reinforced that he had to consider his listeners, not his anxiety. This guy loved conversing and he was quite good at it. It turned out to be just the recommendation he needed. His sales subsequently soared. And on some evenings he was able to return to a community theatre stage with ease.

Tips for Television Appearances

1. Remember that you are in front of your audience to have a conversation with them, not to make some boring, stiff, monotone presentation. If you're unsure as to how to achieve this, practice your conversation on video when you're alone with the material and the camera.

2. Since your audience does not have your written notes in front of them, their minds must perform the work of organizing what you are saying. This is especially true during a TV interview. Make the audience's job easy by enumerating key points and using expressions like "for instance" and "for example."

3. If you are interviewed on a hostile topic, don't ever say, "No comment." That will raise the ire of the interviewer. Instead, say, "We're still gathering the facts" or "Our research to find out what happened will take a few weeks."

4. Rehearse 3 main points you want to explain to your audience through the interviewer. No matter where the conversation goes, be sure to get to these points. Also include the timing and significance of your topic, and an aspect of human interest that will pull heartstrings.

5. Occasionally lean toward the interviewer when you're emphasizing key content. Consider that social media is

very much part of your story, so your image might be longer lasting than your actual interview.

6. Wear bright colors that pop. Avoid pastels, white, and tiny prints that "bleed" on screen and drive audience's eyes crazy.

7. Watch the show before you appear. Will the clothes you intend to wear be comfortable? Will your legs be visible? If so, will your dress hike up? Will your tie be so busy it will distract from what you're saying? Will your bold colors clash with the set's background? The only way you'll know the answers to these questions is to prepare for them in advance.

8. Keep your conversation going as you look at the interviewer, not at the camera, unless you need to make an emphatic point with viewers at home.

9. Avoid long-winded responses to the interviewer's questions. Rehearse in advance quick and meaningful sound bites and pithy stories.

10. You can never rehearse too much. Review, review, review—and even try on clothes at home and watch yourself on video or in a mirror as you get across each of your points.

AMPLIFIER 24

RADIO OR PODCAST INTERVIEWS

When I published my first book, "Don't Bet on the Prince!," my publisher booked me on a radio show on a New York flagship station. The radio host was the childhood actor and comedian from The Partridge Family, Danny Bonaduce. As I advise my clients, I showed up in person with book in hand, in case the station never received the book my publisher sent. (In the media, recognize that Murphy's Law always looms, so we can never be too prepared.)

Danny and I had never met, and I figured redhead to redhead should be fun. When I walked into the studio, the actor had my book, which I was glad to see. But then, as we began to converse, presumably in an attempt to be comedic, he began to rip one page after another out of it. I was flabbergasted as my words fell to the floor, and I thought how disrespectful this was. But we were live on air, so I kept my cool, and the audience never picked up my chagrin.

Months later, I read that the actor had entered rehab for a 25-year battle with alcohol. Media guests never know the people we will meet and what they're going through. Similarly, we never know what nasty callers on a call-in radio show will say. Larger stations have screeners who purge potential potty mouths before they get on air. But even if any slide by, guests must keep calm no matter what, because listeners always remember how you react.

Tips for Radio or Podcast Interviews

1. Use more smiles than you might use ordinarily because the audience can hear a smile in your voice. However, smiling too much will raise the pitch of your voice, and you'll sound powerless and insincere. So, rehearse your projection until you're satisfied with the pitch of the sound you hear.

2. Use varied vocal intonation rather than monotone responses to keep your audience engaged.

3. Try to be in studio for a radio or podcast interview instead of doing the interview from your phone. In person, you can immediately react to an interviewer's body language with your words, and have a livelier conversation. However, current times, expenses, and logistics have made being in studio with your host nearly impossible. To compensate for missing out on a face-to-face interaction with your interviewer, prepare memorable buzz words and expressions that are "vivid" in the pictures they paint.

4. If your radio or podcast interview will be a long one, acknowledge that the listening audience drops in and out. So, repeat key points several times during the show.

AMPLIFIER 25

PRINT OR DIGITAL QUOTES

Newspapers and magazines, including the tabloids, have been calling me for expert quotes for decades. For the most part, I have been quoted accurately. Perhaps that's because if a reporter asks about a particular celebrity, I don't discuss the celebrity per se, but rather the problem I am told that person is facing.

Typically, I say, "When someone has this issue, she is . . ." and I fill in the blanks. This approach works well for me and for the publication: They get to quote someone with my expertise and recognizability, and they promote my brand and my books. Also, by following this technique, I don't cross the line by "psychoanalyzing" people I never met or worked with.

As much as I think this is a good technique, one time this approach didn't work. A tabloid asked me about the beautiful actress Charlize Theron's disciplining of one of her children. I offered my usual response with, "Parents have to set boundaries for their children by. . ."

I thought the interview went fine. Many people don't know the writer of a tabloid story does not create the headline for that story; distant editors do. In this case, editors created what was interpreted as a derogatory headline about the actress' childrearing. I never said anything of the sort. But because I was the expert quoted in the story, readers believed I did.

What followed was a storm of anger aimed at me from the actress' fans. I was not pleased with the news outlet, and I told them so. As a result, for a long while after that, before any of my quotes were published, the tabloid in question routinely ran them by me beforehand. Experts are never given this privilege, but this outlet wanted to maintain the long-standing relationship they had with me.

Be careful what you say and how you say it. You usually won't see your name in print until you read the story after it's published. There is always the possibility that you will be disappointed or offended about how your words were interpreted. Once words are in print, there's little you can do about the copy, but digital errors on the Internet can immediately be corrected. Fortunately, if you ever get caught on the wrong side of a controversy, recognize that outrageous media stories usually blow over within a few days.

Tips for Print or Digital Quotes

1. Prepare your key points in advance, although we never know where a reporter will go in the interview with his questioning.

2. News stories live by the adage, "If it bleeds, it leads." Reporters are after controversy and gore. To be sure it's not *your* controversy or *your* gore, recognize that everything is on the record, even if a reporter promises otherwise.

3. Use humor when you can, but always avoid sarcasm, because it can't be captured in words, and it will usually be translated in an unflattering way.

AMPLIFIER 26

VIDEO CONFERENCE CALLS

The boom of Zoom and other such platforms during the worldwide pandemic allowed many businesses to carry on and survive. But the kind of hiring companies needed to do was different. In the past, tech companies especially were fixated on acquiring staff with high IQs from top schools. But changing business formats quickly required employees with high EQ (Emotional Quotients) who would calmly demonstrate a facility to communicate well, listen carefully, observe insightfully, and act expertly.

I saw a poster that explained the difference, without actually naming IQ or EQ: "Knowledge is knowing what to say" (that's IQ), and "Wisdom is knowing when to say it" (that's EQ). Some people with great knowledge fall flat in social settings because they lack wisdom to appropriately work the room. IQ is an intellectual skill; EQ is a social skill. A good balance of the two is usually preferred. But in cutthroat business settings, which do you think will win?

Entrepreneur Magazine found that 90% of high performers have high EQ. After years of pandemic juggling, however, businesses have learned. Forbes suggested that agility to adapt should be the next new skill required for success. Such agility mandates high EQ. Inc. Magazine suggested that strategic agility be made a corporate priority!

Were workers prepared for these instant alterations? Entrepreneur Magazine noted that while IQ scores have risen by 25 points in recent years, adults' EQ scores have dropped. It was found that only 54% of the United States is emotionally aware, and our country only ranks 15th in EQ. This lack was reflected in the emotional burnout we observed when Video Conference Calls punctured our work/life balance.

To manage companies' new needs, Kelli Nguyen, Editor at LinkedIn News, said that experts predict that post-pandemic managers' roles will shift from authoritarian figure and move toward nurturing mentor. Bosses will need to provide emotional support, as they take on social-emotional oversight to build trust, foster engagement, and motivate collaboration. Is this because few employees have high EQ skills? Whatever the reason, at this point, if companies want to compete successfully, this will be the new corporate mandate.

Joe Cumello, author of the Fast Company article, "How to Hire for Emotional Intelligence during Covid-19," lists high EQ traits as listening, observing, and reading the room; adjusting communications as needed; assessing and reacting to nonverbal cues; knowing when to pause or stop; and motivating through empathy and emotion. These are the necessary skills that support a presenter's media presence. And they are observable through a speaker's emotional reactions, eye contact, and meaningful contribution.

Cool adaptability to new ways of working and relationship-building punctuate EQ. Cumello suggests corporate interviews for new hires include such out-of-the-box questions as, "While making a presentation, you notice some of your listeners reading their emails. What do you do?"

Tips for Video Conference Calls

1. Acknowledge that your first chance may be your *only* chance to impress. The sudden onset of pandemic workarounds alerted employees that visual presence would make or break their careers. For the first time, new emphasis was placed on visual projection. Since video calls are often recorded, the impression employees make can be studied, and will linger.

2. Always use professional lighting. I have a ring light for standing, and a desk ring light for Zoom-type calls when I'm seated. Sometimes, I use both at the same time. Poor lighting casts unwanted shadows by which no one should be remembered. Besides, when employees go out of their way to equip make-shift offices with professional production tools, it suggests their willingness to go out of their way to also do their jobs. Bosses notice the engagement of their employees, especially in light of past studies about poor employee engagement.

3. Test your equipment with friends *before* your professional video calls. Determine what works best for you and your equipment in your make-shift office. Many people use external microphones. I purchased an external Yeti mic, but my rehearsal partners all say they hear me clearly without it. Consequently, I have been able to stick with the mic built into my computer. The operative words here are "rehearse beforehand."

4. Dress well for your calls. Perhaps not as formally as you would in your office, remember that you are still making an impression even if you're at home. It's worth repeating that although you're sure your viewers won't see what's beneath your torso, that attire does support your body language above your waist, so take heed! Belgium's Antwerp mayor was

caught on a live-streamed Zoom call interview in his underwear. He didn't intentionally flash his undies, but he was sitting with a mirror behind him! Carefully consider not only what's in front of you on your computer screen, but also what's surrounding you from every angle.

5. As much as possible, set up a private and quiet section of your house to conduct your business. One woman said she did her video calls out of her junk closet. But she looked and sounded so professional, nobody knew — or cared.

6. For entrepreneurs, create backgrounds that signify your brand. I created different backgrounds with each of my different books. While I was doing a Zoom interview for one company, a participant took the book title that was showing over my head and quoted it onto Twitter, as though it was one of my discussion points: "Don't lie on your back for a guy who doesn't have yours"-- with full attribution of my name. That became an unexpected perk for me as I delivered my information on Zoom. So, think of your brand's background as your personal billboard. All you have to do is show up with your background behind you, and you'll reap the benefits of free additional advertising!

AMPLIFIER 27

PART 5--FINALE
What's Your Strongest Platform?

There is no excuse for not being prepared for every media interaction you have. Be yourself and converse like you're talking with a friend. Avoid negativity, smile, attach non-forced humor when possible, and contribute unique information. Light yourself well, dress respectfully, and tell yourself you will nail your goal.

More than anything else, recognize that YOU are in charge. One morning, I awoke to my phone ringing nonstop. Nothing unusual, a media outlet was again calling for me to offer my expertise on a celebrity's behavior. But I was shocked when the reporter I knew for years told me that this time the story was about me. "Me?," I questioned. The reporter explained: Actress Sienna Miller had been going through a rough patch with her latest love. She told press sources they worked things out, thanks to her getting relationship counseling from Dr. Gilda Carle. What? I immediately checked the Internet, and it was on fire with this story published around the world, from New York to India.

I would never share names of people I counsel. In fact, one Baywatch beauty told me she preferred engaging with me on the Internet because Hollywood paparazzi follow celebs into their therapists' offices to track their private lives!

Now the media wanted to get details about my counseling the actress. I told them I would never divulge with whom I work. They insisted, and I stood my ground. I was called to appear on Access Hollywood, where I maintained there was no story.

The media wanted to get the juicy details about my allegedly counseling the actress. I told them I would never divulge with whom I work. They insisted, and I stood my ground. I was called to appear on Access Hollywood, where I maintained there was no story. Cameras were rolling. The entertainment reporter told me it was okay if I didn't want to SAY this information directly. But he asked me to nod my head if it was true, and he'd accept that. I repeated there was no story here. He tried for 20 minutes, and soon I left. They were disappointed they were unable to get this scoop.

Remember that you are totally in charge every time you are interviewed. No one can push you to say anything you don't want to say. But also remember the media provides great opportunities for you to sell your brand.

All you have to do is learn these platforms, practice with them as often as you can, and then amplify your brand with ease. Don't limit your visual presence to only one platform. Be adroit on all the platforms, because you never know when you'll be called upon to use one with which you're less familiar.

Of the 4 platforms we discussed above, which is the one you feel strongest using? Why? With which do you need to develop greater skills? Why?

My friend, Dr. Diane Hamilton, has a refreshing quest for knowledge. She decidedly plunges into whatever task she most dislikes doing. If one of these platforms were less of a favorite for her, she'd study it, practice using it, and become expert in it.

Most people would run the other way from difficulties. I witnessed someone who refused to toast his sister at her wedding as had been planned, because he couldn't bring himself to speak in public. Where did that get him? More people should adapt Dr. Diane's drive not to run from an unsavory task, but to embrace it and work to become skilled at it. Today, Diane has a brilliant worldwide reputation as a behavioral strategist, while this guy has become withdrawn and bitter.

Since the demand for polished media presence is here to stay, it's your choice to be bitter or better. Which do you prefer?

PART 6
ORGANIZING YOUR MESSAGE

AMPLIFIER 28

INTRODUCTION TO YOUR CONTENT

Know your audience's needs and goals
IN ADVANCE.

Use one of these HOOKS to immediately grab your audience's attention:

1. Relate an experience or humorous story relevant to your information.

2. Refer to the occasion, audience, or reason for your being there.

3. Refer to the subject, its timeliness, its importance.

4. Build a dramatic situation to establish background for the statement of your THESIS.

5. Use an illustration.

6. State an arresting fact.

7. Prompt audience involvement by asking for feedback.

DO NOT:

1. Give your audience credit for knowing more or less about the subject than they do.

2. Tell stories irrelevant to the subject.

3. Tell stories irrelevant to the subject.

4. Tell stories that do not have a point to them.

5. Destroy confidence by making apologies.

6. Use an introduction that is too long.

AMPLIFIER 29

THESIS

YOUR CENTRAL THOUGHT

The THESIS belongs at the end of the INTRODUCTION, but before the BODY of your presentation.

The THESIS should be a one-sentence statement that TELLS THE AUDIENCE WHAT YOU WILL TELL THEM.

The THESIS should be stated at least **3 TIMES** throughout your appearance, in different ways, using different words.

AMPLIFIER 30

TRANSITION

Since listeners' minds wander, use TRANSITIONS to grab them back!

Where should transitions be used?
  --from INTRODUCTION to THESIS
  --from THESIS to MAIN IDEA #1
  --from MAIN IDEA #1 to each supporting DETAIL
  --from last supporting DETAIL to MAIN IDEA #2
  --from last supporting DETAIL to CONCLUSION

<u>Different Kinds of Transitions</u>

1. WORDS OF TRANSITION: "therefore," "because," "Today I want to discuss…," "first, second, third…"

2. PAUSE

3. VOCAL CHANGE

4. GESTURE

5. MOVEMENT

Each transition should include:
restatement of the THESIS and/or a reference to the preceding point

Read the following passage aloud, with deliberate emphasis on the bolded transitions:

Money may be an evil, **but** it is **also** an essential. We can't get along without it, no matter how hard we try. We need it for food, shelter, clothing, medical care, **and** everything else that sustains our life. **In addition**, we need it for fun—for travel, for music, for sports, **and** for entertainment with friends. **Perhaps most important**, we need it psychologically, as evidence of our personal competence in today's world. **So**, don't disregard the folding stuff as totally evil, **even though** the quest for it may lead, in some cases, to tension **and** to crime.

How did you feel reading this passage with these bolded emphases?

DR. GILDA CARLE

AMPLIFIER 31

WORDS OF TRANSITION

ADDITION:
> in addition, furthermore, moreover, also, equally important

EXAMPLE:
> for example, for instance, thus, in other words, as an illustration, in particular

SUGGESTION:
> for this purpose, to this end, with this object

EMPHASIS:
> indeed, truly, again, to repeat, in fact

MAKING A POINT:
> granted that, although, though, even though, while it may be true, in spite of

SUMMARY:
> in summary, in conclusion, therefore, finally, consequently, thus, accordingly, in short, as a result, on the whole

SEQUENCE:
> first, second, third…, then, once, after, next, subsequently, previously, at last, meanwhile, in the meantime, immediately, soon, at length, when, yesterday, today, tomorrow, above, across, under, beyond, below, nearly, opposite to, to the left, to the right

RELATIONSHIP:
similarly, likewise, in the same way, however, in contrast to, but, still, nevertheless, yet, conversely, notwithstanding, on the other hand, on the contrary, at the same time, while this may be true, consequently, because, since, therefore, accordingly, thus, hence, due to, as a result

AMPLIFIER 32

BODY

The BODY develops the THESIS so that:
    --it keeps the audience interested
    --key points are remembered

The BODY tells the audience what you promised to tell them in the THESIS.

The BODY consists of Main Ideas, each of which has supporting details.

The objective of the BODY is to **Encompass**, **Enlighten**, and **Enthuse** the audience.

The BODY includes:
    pictures, photos, transparencies, names of persons, places, and things, music or other sound effects, dates, comparisons, expert testimony, quotes, and statistics to illustrate key points.

AMPLIFIER 33

INCORPORATING VISUAL AIDS

<u>Visual Aids may include:</u>
models, samples, slides, printed pictures, photos, diagrams, videos, graphs, charts, maps, cartoons, posters, movies, flip charts, and more

Visuals must ENHANCE your appearance,
NOT COMPETE with it.

STEPS FOR USING VISUALS

1. Outline your presentation. Decide where a visual aid will add emphasis, clarity, and/or additional information.

2. Show each visual only when needed.

3. Show each visual long enough for full comprehension. Then remove it.

4. Written visuals should reflect only ONE idea.

5. Rehearse your presentation with all visuals for smooth and natural transition.

6. Count on Murphy's Law ("what *can* go wrong *will* go wrong") and create a contingency plan if a visual cannot be used.

7. Keep lights bright while showing visuals so audience doesn't doze off.

8. Use the <u>3 T's for Visuals</u>: TOUCH the visual, TURN to the audience, and TALK to the audience, never to the visuals.

9. Do not weaken your CONCLUSION by starting to pack up your visuals while you are speaking.

10. When closing your presentation, move away from your visuals and speak directly to your audience.

AMPLIFIER 34

CONCLUSION TO YOUR CONTENT

The CONCLUSION must:

--TELL THE AUDIENCE WHAT YOU TOLD THEM throughout your appearance

--restate the key points, preferably in different ways

--relate the key points to the THESIS

--integrate the key points with the needs and goals of the audience

--make the THESIS memorable

--command action or reaction from your audience

**Like the end of a pencil,
the CONCLUSION *must make a point*!
The point should ACCENTUATE YOUR BRAND.**

Suggestions:

1. Use references to your audience to increase likeability for you and your THESIS.

2. Use a final, memorable example or illustration to Amplify your THESIS.

DR. GILDA CARLE

<u>AMPLIFIER 35</u>

PART 4--FINALE
Good Structure Sustains Engagement

For a segment I did called "Dating Terms in 2020," instead of the traditional Introduction, Body, and Conclusion for each presentation, this interviewer chose to use a countdown:
https://www.youtube.com/watch?v=lbjK6yW2n1Y

There were 7 points I was prepared to discuss, but the interviewer only picked 4. I could have presented my information by enumerating every point and delivering the facts without embellishment. But that's not my style—and speakers must keep to their personality to remain believable.

Before the segment, the interviewer shared that her goal was to have a light morning exchange to celebrate the new year. So, I planned on incorporating plenty of laughs.

The organization of the message was easy to follow, as enumeration generally is. For each numbered point, there was a distinct Introduction, Body, and Conclusion. Frankly, I thought this was a silly segment, but the new year was meant to be joyful. Now I'm glad we had so much fun that day, because just a few months later, our world was rocked by the coronavirus pandemic, riots, racial discord, and plenty of deaths.

Moral of This Story: Enjoy life's belly laughs when they come, because such opportunities disappear quickly!

Note how my style here is to avoid a stiff *presentation* in

favor of an engaging, fluid *conversation*. I also apply the technique
of providing examples and definitions after I make each point.

I used my book title as an example for one of my points, while it also reminded us both that it was sitting there until the interviewer became ready for it. (Backstory: She must have been deeply engaged, because the host snatched the book to read at home!)

1. This interview ran 5 minutes, 19 seconds. After watching the shorter videos, were you able to remain focused on this longer one? Why or why not?

2. What will you remember about this segment?

3. What would you have liked to see me change?

4. What would you do differently if you were on screen?

PART 7
APPLYING YOUR MESSAGE

AMPLIFIER 36

PURPOSES OF YOUR PRESENTATION

Each speaking engagement has <u>2 MAJOR PURPOSES</u>:

--to <u>INFORM</u> --through a clear description, demonstration, or explanation

--to <u>PERSUADE</u> --with your idea or concept

<u>Different Types of Outlines</u>
--full sentence
--key phrase
--key word

Incorporate the type of outline with which you feel most comfortable. But you won't know your preferred type unless you rehearse all of them — with full sentences, key phrases, and key words. Caution: The more words you have in front of you, the greater the chance you'll use them as a crutch, and if you're nervous, read them. When you read in front of an audience, you lose eye contact with your audience, and they drop out.

So decide in advance what your preferred outline type is, and rehearse your delivery many times in private.

DR. GILDA CARLE

AMPLIFIER 37

SPEECH OUTLINE

Clip the takeaway on the next page and have it with you when you plan each presentation.

SPEECH OUTLINE
PUTTING IT ALL TOGETHER

INTRODUCTION
(Engage)

- **HOOK** _____

- **THESIS** *"Today I'm going to tell you about..."* _____

BODY
(Encompass, Enlighten, Enthuse)

- **MAIN IDEA #1** _____

    Supporting Detail (a) _____
    (Examples, Visuals)

    Supporting Detail (b) _____

    Transition _____

- **MAIN IDEA #2** _____

    Supporting Detail (a) _____
    (Examples, Visuals)

    Supporting Detail (b) _____

    Transition _____

CONCLUSION
(Enlist)

- **SUMMARY** *"Today I told you about..."* _____

www.DrGilda.com

AMPLIFIER 38

EXTRA MEDIA SECRETS

1. When being in the media, always employ my **S-O-F-A Technique**: **S**mile, **O**pen Posture, **F**orward Lean, and **A**cknowledge your interviewer.

2. Follow the **50/50 EYE-ALOGUE Rule**: When you are being interviewed in front of an audience, direct 50% of your eye-alogue to the person asking the questions, and 50% to the rest of the audience. If you're being interviewed without an audience, direct 100% of your *attention* to your interviewer, but don't stare! Have a cordial *conversation* with your interviewer as you would with a friend.

3. **REPEAT** or **PARAPHRASE** intense questions, always making *your* response positive. This allows your audience to hear the question again, it buys you time to determine which part of the question to address and how, and it gives you pause to diffuse heated emotions.

4. When responding to a question, use the **PROBLEM/SOLUTION FORMAT**:
    a. The Problem is…
    b. The Solution is…
    c. Here are the Details…

5. Apply this **PACING TECHNIQUE** to personalize your responses to questions:
    a. Mirror your questioner's body language and words, if possible.

b. Avoid repeating negative buzz words.
   c. Always employ a conversational tone.

6. Tell a **HOSTILE QUESTIONER** you're happy to discuss the topic with her after the show. Disengage eye-alogue, smile, and change to a different and positive topic. Never take negative comments personally. Some media people think negativity will get them higher ratings. Disengage from that. Don't let the audience or interviewer see you respond with negativity. Rise above it.

7. Respond to all Questions positively (even when you may want to bash the interviewer!)

8. Your listeners want you to succeed. Prove to them you're cool, no matter what the noise around you is!

9. If you can, leave your audience hanging onto some suspenseful point, so they're hungry for MORE from you. To be invited back would be perfect!

AMPLIFIER 39

SPEAKER'S CHECKLIST

Information not heard as you delivered it is NOT information at all!

1. Body Language & Voice Are 93% of Your Message!

2. Audience Focus:
    A. Ho Hum...
    B. What's In It For Me?
    C. For Example?
    D. So What?

3. Speaker's Objective:
    A. Motivate
    B. Communicate
    C. Illustrate
    D. Activate

4. Speaker's Approach:
    A. Engage
    B. Encompass
    C. Enlighten
    D. Enthuse
    E. Enlist

5. Speaker's Technique:
    A. Hook
    B. Appeal
    C. Exemplify
    D. Command

AMPLIFIER 40

STAR IN YOUR OWN COMMERCIAL

Most TV commercials are 30 seconds long. You'll be surprised how much can fit into 30 seconds when your message is well-designed. Watch 3 different commercials on 3 different networks. What were your impressions?

Note how each commercial HOOK for your attention was immediate and quick. It's the commercial's job to get a *reaction* from you. The brand that sponsors each commercial wants your reaction to be positive so you buy what they're selling. Can you think of a time that a brand's commercial was so successful in moving *you* that you altered your buying habits to own it?

Gilda-Gram®
Your objective is to be
REMEMBERED and REFERRED.

On your cell phone, videotape yourself selling yourself to someone. You have 30 seconds. This exercise is merely for you to feel how long 30 seconds is. Watch the playback. If someone didn't know you, would they *remember* you? Would they *refer* you? Try it a few different times and ways. How successful do you think you were? Why?

Supplemental Reading: To discover more about your media presence, read "Don't Bet on the Prince!," (by Dr. Gilda Carle), especially Chapter 3, "Ask for What You Need and Believe You Deserve to Get It" and Chapter 4, "Project a Power Image."

AMPLIFIER 41

PART 7--FINALE
Prepare for Unusual Happenings

I was being interviewed to discuss the celebrities in the news who had bribed scammers to get their kids into prestigious colleges. Instead, it became a discussion about parenting. I've worked with this very generous interviewer before. (You'll see why I say this.) I prepared my soundbites thoroughly, recognizing they might be discarded because he's verbose.

During my first interview with him, I wondered if he'd let me speak. This segment turned out to be a deep interchange, with the host's unexpectedly lengthy promotion for my book. See "Too Much Parenting"-- **https://www.youtube.com/watch?v=ciMaAlbehBs**

One of the aspects of applying your message during a live interview is that you have to be aware of many things *at once*. You must know your content, of course, but you must also be willing to discard it if the timing doesn't work. *No one can know about timing in advance.* But when you're comfortable with your information, expertise, and persona, you'll appear confident and knowledgeable.

I was a regular on Good Day New York. While being interviewed by the host, an aging musician with hearing problems was to be interviewed next. While the host and I were conversing, the musician neared the stage too soon, he tripped, and there was a crashing noise. It riled the host, and he froze. But we were live, so I kept yapping as though nothing had occurred. The grateful host returned to our conversation within a few seconds, and we were back on track. *During live interviews, anything can happen, so expect that many anythings will (Murphy's Law again!).*

1. The above interview ran 4 minutes, 1 second. Did it keep your interest? Why?

2. What will you remember about this segment?

3. What would you have liked to see me change?

4. What would you do differently if you were on screen?

PART 8
OPTIMIZING YOUR MESSAGE

AMPLIFIER 42

REHEARSING YOUR PRESENTATION

Rehearsing is merely thinking out loud.

Your rehearsal must contain **2 Parts**:

1. **Introspective Rehearsal**
    a. Think about what is to be said.
    b. Memorize the *patterns* of the presentation.
    c. Mentally review specific planned behavior.
    d. Memorize specific buzz words and sound bites.
    e. Memorize specific items of information.

2. **Auditory Rehearsal**
    a. Rehearse on video or in front of knowledgeable listeners who are not emotionally involved with you.
    b. Request honest feedback about how your presentation looks, sounds, and flows.
    c. After your presentation, ask your informal observers:
        --What points do you remember?
        --Would you remember these points in 2 days? 2 weeks? 2 months?

It's dangerous to memorize! Under stress, you can go blank. Instead, rehearse and review so you know your content thoroughly. Above all, believe in yourself! A diamond was a chunk of coal that did well under pressure. Welcome the pressure, and vow that you'll become that diamond!

REHEARSE . . . . . REHEARSE . . . . . REHEARSE . . . . .

AMPLIFIER 43

10 INTERVIEW MISTAKES --and HOW TO FIX THEM

MISTAKE #1
You don't give your full name and title to the reporter. Consequently, the screen misspells your name or gets your title wrong.
THE FIX
If a reporter doesn't know you, he may ask you to say your name on camera, spell it, and say your title. This information goes on tape so the newsroom gets it right. However, there can be mistakes in your name's pronunciation, its spelling, or even your title. I have had to casually, with a smile, correct a host in a gentle way. It's okay if it's done kindly.

MISTAKE #2
You continuously say your web address during a live interview.
THE FIX
When you keep name-dropping your URL, it's a turn-off to the audience, the reporter, and your goal of getting that free press you're after. You're there as an expert to disseminate FREE information. If you're a great guest, the reporter may naturally ask, "How can people get in touch with you?" That's your URL cue, and so much more graceful. Remember to TELL when asked, rather than SELL throughout your interview.

MISTAKE #3
When the interviewer continues to press you on the same question and you're exasperated. You look impatient and keep repeating phrases like "again" and "as I said."
THE FIX
An experienced reporter may ask you the same question several times to offer you more chances to sound compelling, or the reporter may be hostile toward you and will try to make this a "got'cha" report where you'll get tripped up and look bad. Each time you answer the *same question*, make it look and sound like it's *brand new*, without allowing your personal feelings to get in the way.

MISTAKE #4
You are intense and serious on camera.
THE FIX
Practice smiling when you talk. It makes you more attractive, and it takes the intensity out of your responses. (This does not apply if you're discussing a serious, life-and-death issue.)

MISTAKE #5
You are rambling and rambling and rambling.
THE FIX
Watch experts in the news. Note what great sound bites they use. Devise a few of your own before being interviewed. Make them compelling 7- to 12-second sound bites. Then practice them and practice and practice.

MISTAKE #6
You find yourself offering many details during a 3-minute interview.
THE FIX
It's your job to supply the passion, excitement, joy, or sadness of your topic. Allow the reporter to tell the details. The reporter usually wears an earpiece with directions from

the studio's control room on how much time there is left. Viewers are attracted to emotion. Example: "After this doctor saved my life, I knew I wanted to become a physician, too. That's exactly what happened." OR "I'm so touched by the attendance tonight. Our community proved it cares about beating diabetes."

MISTAKE #7
You are not answering the reporter's questions during your interview. This may be an intentional technique if a reporter is hostile. Most are not. Listen carefully to what you're being asked, and respond appropriately. Listening is the nicest thing you can demonstrate during an interview. The second nicest thing is your response.
THE FIX
Reporters often write their story before they show up for your interview. So, during your interview, let the reporter *tell you what to say*. Example: Reporter: "Look at the huge crowd of people at your event!" You: "Yes. More than 5,000 people showed up, and we expect more before the night is over. We're thrilled. Thank you, everyone!"

MISTAKE #8
You are looking at the camera, rather than at the reporter asking the questions.
THE FIX
Have a real *conversation* with your interviewer. If you continue to stare into the camera, it's disrespectful to your conversational partner, and the audience reads you as primping and ego-driven. That's a sure way to end your media career.

MISTAKE #9
You find that you're wearing the wrong clothes or accessories on camera.

THE FIX
Wear bright colors. Avoid muted tones, small patterns, white or pastels, and noisy jewelry. Also, try on your outfit before appearing to be sure it fits comfortably.

MISTAKE #10
You neglected to send a thank-you note after your interview.
THE FIX
After a TV or radio interview, send a thank-you note to the reporter or host or producer. That small kindness may get you to be asked back, the highest compliment of a media interview.

***

Questions? Other Mistakes? Check-ups?
Ask Dr. Gilda at www.DrGilda.com

AMPLIFIER 44

BODY LANGUAGE SPOKEN HERE

Our body posture speaks a language all its own. It accounts for 55% of the impression we make on others. It indicates to our audience how we feel about ourselves. Posture that suggests we can be pushed around will hold us back. A body that announces we are forces of strength will re-enforce our power.

We can all interpret body language if we choose to recognize its true meaning. Unnatural, disjointed movements may indicate a sense of conflict; slumped posture and shuffling movements may indicate depression or alienation; frantic, rushed movements may indicate stress or anxiety. If we choose to acknowledge the meanings behind the body language of the people we meet, we can avoid setting ourselves up for disappointment, and instead pursue more enriched relationships. Our body language communicates how much power we have, and how much power we command.

Because this is such a vital tool that escapes most people's formal education, I created a program called "How to Project a Power Image" that I conducted throughout the United States for corporate executives, salespeople, women's groups, and graduate business students. It was such a popular workshop, some open-to-the-public events had standing room only. And weeks later, a few attendees reached out to me to report that their new, more positive body language earned them promotions and raises!

The power in the language of body emanates from the center of gravity, the pelvis. This is the focus of our energy, the point where balance and poise connect. Masters of karate, aikido, Sumo wrestling, tai chi and dance emanate from this center. The body must be aligned with a lengthened spine and a head held high. The pelvis is tucked underneath. An imaginary string runs through the body, similar to that of a marionette. Powerful people use focused body posture. As a result, they can then focus their full attention on what they are saying.

The interest in projecting power posture is increasing. The scientific art of Rolfing realigns the body and releases tightness in the connective tissue through deep massage. It has gained much attention in recent years. In the 1988 movie "Crossing Delancey," elderly ladies in New York City learned power walking techniques as a form of self-protection against street muggers. Power posture emits the message, "Don't mess with me." It also transmits the bulletin to organizational decisionmakers, "I am moving up." Ultimately, it issues the statement to the world at large, "I am strong, I am in control."

Power posture energizes a person and commands attention as well, even during a nerve-racking interview. Some of my clients are often questioned by the media. They sit before the critical eye of a TV camera that can pan their every weakness. Because the interview is such a stressful event for even the most seasoned participant, I developed the **S-O-F-A Technique** that I mentioned earlier, for enunciating your power. Now let's delve into it.

Whether a person is sitting or standing, employing the S-O-F-A will make the difference between power projection and audience rejection.

This S-O-F-A Has 4 Pillows

1. **S**: <u>Smile</u>.
You are never fully dressed unless you wear a smile. In his book, "Telling Lies," Paul Ekman catalogues over 50 different smiles that people use. A genuine smile affects the whole face, especially the crow's feet areas of the eyes. Insincere smiles are asymmetrical, inappropriately timed, and last longer than a few seconds. Be sure your smile is genuine. Come on! It only takes 12 muscles to smile, while it takes 42 muscles to frown. Besides, imagine how many fewer wrinkles smiling will generate!

2. **O**: <u>Open your posture</u>.
Much research has been conducted about the way powerful people use space. In nearly all cultures, high status people take up more space than low status people. In corporations, high status employees are granted desirable and spatial physical workspaces, such as the proverbial corner office. Men and extroverts occupy more space than women and introverts. And women's space tends to be intruded upon more often than men's.

Note how differently men and women sitting at a meeting use their space. Women's skirts prevent them from crossing their legs in the same position that men use. As a consequence, women sit more tightly than their male counterparts. As for the upper limbs, note how men spread their arms onto a chair next to them more so than women.

At a workshop on Body Language I conducted with executives of a successful technology company, I pointed to the casual way one man in the class was sitting. He was spread out, with his chair tipped back as far as it would go while his arms were crossed behind his neck. I noted to the group how dominant his use of space was. The group laughed as they informed me that he was the president of their company! Rank does occupy more space!

At a workshop on Body Language I conducted with executives of a successful technology company, I pointed to the casual way one man in the class was sitting. He was spread out, with his chair tipped back as far as it would go while his arms were crossed behind his neck. I noted to the group how dominant his use of space was. The group laughed as they informed me that he was the president of their company! Rank does occupy more space!

To project a Power Image, take up space. Mark your dominion by extending your limbs: reach out while sitting, become more expansive while standing.

3. **F**: <u>Forward Lean</u>.
Sit on the bones of your buttocks, with your back away from your chair. Become higher and larger than you would if you were comfortably positioned in your seat. Lean towards your listener (or speaker) to let her know that you are listening or speaking to her at the highest Critical Listening step on the listening hierarchy.

4. **A**: <u>Acknowledge your Listener</u>.
Use head nodding to indicate your acceptance, your interest, and your like for the person doing the speaking. The nicest thing two people can do for one another is to ACKNOWLEDGE each other's value.

On your chair right now, use the S-O-F-A Technique to visually expand your territory. If you have a video available, note how you appear when your body is contracted. Compare that with how you look when your body is extended. When some people open their images, they can look twice their actual size.

Especially during an interview, if at all possible, shorter people should sit on a chair higher than their listener. If appropriate, and if they feel comfortable, they might try standing to make important points, even while listeners remain seated. I coach one diminutive saleswoman who purposely gets out of her chair to come around to where her potential client is seated at his desk. She deliberately stands over him and points to some information in the literature she has brought. She does it in a nonthreatening manner, but her potential client can feel this "little lady" is in command. Your body posturing can subliminally influence a client who is considering entrusting a major account to you!

Power projection includes keeping your chin raised. The expression, "Keep your chin up" is meant to advise people to demonstrate their greatest power in their lower face region. Visualize Sherman's "power chin" in the 1987 movie Bonfire of the Vanities; I counted at least 15 references author Tom Wolf used as an allegory to this character's noble jaw.

Part of power posture involves the use of our hands. While the face has only 14 bones, each hand has 27. It can operate as a level, a crowbar, a wrench. It can function as a caresser or an aggressor. The Bible mentions the *hand* of God over 1,400 times; we, ourselves judge others as high-*handed*, even-*handed*, heavy-*handed*, or under*handed*. We point the finger of accusation, we keep our finger on the pulse, but we deliver "the finger" to those we accuse. And be careful, because our hands tattle on our innermost power: they tremble when we are anxious, they grow cold with our fear, they hide behind us in our shame, they twist in our anguish.

The hands also reveal our touching privileges. The power of touch is very strong. We judge people quickly by their handshakes. Would you want to do business with a limp fish? Or would you prefer to know your business will be "well-handled"? Hands hold the language of physical intimacy. They send messages of union and communion. Routinely, we make business decisions on the nature of a person's handshake. One time, after I shook the hand of someone I contemplated hiring to create a powerful brochure for me, I decided against her. Her handshake was the proverbial "limp fish." I needed a powerful designer for the project, and based on her handshake, I surmised that this woman was not.

Rank has its touching privileges. High status people in corporations and those with dominant personalities enjoy special touch liberties with their lower status subordinates. Low status employees are touched more than high status employees. Children are touched more than adults. Women are touched more often and on more parts of their body than men. During this time of so many harassment accusations and lawsuits, people have become more aware of limiting their reaching out.

Researchers find that it is harder to say "No" to a request that is accompanied by a touch. Imagine your boss putting his or her hand on your shoulder while speaking to you. Can you fathom the reverse, with you placing your hand on your boss' shoulder? Most people cannot.

In this case, touching privileges, rank, and gender seem not to be related. I have observed female executives put their hand on the shoulder of a male subordinate, although he would never think to do a similar thing to his female boss. By the same token, I have seen male bosses do the same with their female subordinates, whereas they would not think to do likewise with their superior.

The 5 Categories of Touch

1. <u>professional</u>: for our doctor, barber, tailor

2. <u>social</u>: for the handshake that can either make or break a deal
3. <u>intimate</u>: for our closest family and friends
4. <u>friendly</u>: for our most caring associates
5. <u>sexual</u>: for our special relationships

Touching privileges are determined by a society's mores. The United States is considered to be a low touch culture. While we love to stroke our house pets, we need to be reminded on our bumper stickers, "Have you hugged your child today?" Asian cultures use less touch, and Mediterranean cultures use more. Within these broad cultural categories, the amount of touch differs among individuals, families, and geographic regions.

Even the touching rules between the genders are different. A study of pre-surgery patients touched by a female nurse showed that women had positive reactions to touch: their blood pressure went down and they experienced less anxiety. In contrast, the men demonstrated increased blood pressure and higher levels of anxiety; it was reasoned that their need to be dependent on a female caretaker made them somewhat uncomfortable.

But we must have touch for our survival. Family therapist Virginia Satir recommended 4 hugs a day for survival, 8 hugs a day for maintenance, and 12 hugs a day for growth. Author Leo Buscaglia settled for 5 hugs a day. Whatever the exact prescription, healthy human infants deprived of touch, cuddling, and stroking for long periods of time face depression, withdrawal, and death.

Elderly people deprived of another's body contact often suffer from "skin hunger." Recently, studies with pets assigned to people in nursing homes have shown improved health outcomes of the patients as they continually touched the furry animals.

Even the distance we use when we communicate projects our power. Edward Hall, in his best-selling book in 1966, The Hidden Dimension, discussed 4 categories of distance that we still use today when we communicate. They are:

>   --<u>intimate space</u>: touching to 18 inches
>   --<u>personal space</u>: 18 inches to 4 feet
>   --<u>social space</u>: 4 feet to 12 feet
>   --<u>public space</u>: 12 feet and more.

Now we can add what we can call "Pandemic Space" of at least 6 feet, and probably more.

Generally, we tend to sit and stand closer to people we feel positive about. A study conducted at Brigham Young University in Utah revealed that the farther husbands stood from their wives, the more dissatisfied they were with their marriages. Couples were asked to walk towards their partners, stop, and talk at a comfortable distance. On average, men who were happily married stood 11.4 inches away from their wives, whereas men who were unhappy stood 14.8 inches away.

Physiologist Dr. Valerie Hunt studied the human energy field, the "aura," that people naturally emit through their bodies. According to her findings, we give off auric color vibrations, sounds, which change in concert with our deepest emotions. The frequency of this aura is from 0 to 200,000 cycles per second. This rate is much higher than the frequency cycles of the heart, brain or muscle contractions which are never more than 1000 cycles per second. As open systems, we mutually infect each other's lives with our auras. As a result, what we project, others reflect.

The power we project through our body language punctuates our sense of self-worth. Others can observe how we are feeling, what we are thinking, and even our reactions to them. If we choose to interpret body language correctly, it can provide us with a wealth of information that will enhance our interactions. Choose to project your power in positive ways, and what you give out, you'll be happy to get back.

Since our body language counts for 55% of the image we project, it is worthwhile to evaluate it on videotape. Turn off the sound and watch your body movements in silence. Would you want to continue communicating with the image you observe? Look for unique ways to emphasize your most positive body movements so as to attract positive feedback from your audience.

Assess your videotaped body language with the characteristics for POWERLESS vs. POWERFUL body expression below:

PowerLESS Body Language
    rounded shoulders
    head down
    eyes downcast
    tightly clasped hands
    slow, shuffle-type walk
    lack of hand gestures
    fiddling with hair, face, pencil
    sticking fingers in mouth

PowerLESS Facial Expressions
    wandering eye movements
    stiff lips
    infrequent smiles
    smiling while speaking seriously

staring into space
stone face
worried face
tight-lipped smile
covering mouth with hand
biting cheek or lip
excessive licking of lips
excessive tongue movements

POWERFUL Body Language

straight shoulders
head erect
relaxed arms and hands
steady, direct stride
straight posture
use of hand gestures
responsive nod of head

POWERFUL Facial Expressions

ready smile
looking directly at listener while conversing
relaxed mouth and face
facial expressions matching the spoken words

You just viewed yourself on screen.

1) Would you hire YOU for a responsible job?

2) Would you invest money in your company?

3) Would you buy your product or service?

4) Would you want you to return for additional conversation?

5) Would you invite you into your home?

6) What you see is what you get. What did you get from viewing your appearance on screen?

Gilda-Gram®
Guide your seer to see you
exactly as you want to be seen.

If you're not happy with the image of yourself you now see, change your body posture. It's a bold 55% of the impact you make on others. Try different body poses. When you feel totally comfortable with one, tape yourself and assess what you see. Study that comfy pose, because you'll want to keep it as your signature projection. Your comfort will automatically comfort your audience. The more comfortable your audience feels with you, the more quickly they will be persuaded to follow you, hire you, buy from you, and read more of your books. YOU are totally in charge!

AMPLIFIER 45

CASE STUDY: BRAND STRATEGY OF A CORPORATE LEADER

Dr. Jo Ivey Boufford, President of New York City Health & Hospitals Corporation

In 1988, I was a young college professor at a small New York college, teaching in the MBA program in its School of Business. I also had a corporate consulting business that trained executives in public presentations, keynote speeches, and media interactions. One of my clients was Jay Richard Goldstein, M.D. who was the Commissioner of Health of New Jersey. He hired me to train his deputies in how to optimize their media exchanges. The training was so effective, Dr. Goldstein asked me to return to "undo" some of the ease I gave them, because a few were calling unnecessary news conferences every day just to be on camera! Dr. Goldstein and I laughed.

One of his friends was Jo Ivey Boufford, M.D., who in 1985 became the first female President of the New York City Health and Hospitals Corporation, the largest municipal system in the United States, overseeing many billions of healthcare dollars. Dr. Boufford was a lovely, personable, bright pediatrician, who was used to dressing casually under her white lab coat, with straggly hair and no makeup. She was unschooled in media interaction and politics, which made her an easy mark for the slick, bullying male politicians running New York City's government. Routinely, they would threaten cutbacks and less funding for her essential services. She clearly needed to do something to level the playing field. With the good track record I had working with his deputies, Dr. Goldstein recommended she contact me at once.

Because our schedules were jam-packed, we worked together for the first time during an entire weekend. I hired hair, makeup, and clothing stylists, while I cram-coursed her with emphatic leadership techniques, assertive body carriage, buzzwords, and media presence essentials, similar to the contents in this book.

After our vigorous weekend, on Monday morning, she was ready to face the aggressive and argumentative New York politicians on the steps of City Hall. Immediately, they were taken aback. Obviously, I had done a great job! She felt empowered, and her new leadership style was unambiguous.

But a few days later, on the front cover of the New York Post, there was a Before and After photo of the doctor, with the scandalous headline that she paid me, a mere "Image Consultant," a lot of money for image consulting while the city's hospitals were strapped for cash. What? There was no mention of my having a legitimate Ph.D. with lots of experience training executives on Wall Street! This was my introduction to nasty, cutthroat media politics.

The backstory—and there's always a backstory—was that she had fired one of the New York City hospital presidents for underperforming, and that person was hellbent on retaliation. The fired employee leaked this story to the newspapers, and it was picked up throughout the country. The New York Inspector General investigated Dr. Boufford and me, to try to make a case that we had billed for illegitimate services. Of course, that investigation went nowhere, because every company invests in training its staff, and this is what we were doing. The truth was that I had actually cut my fees from my usual corporate contracts in an effort to serve this client. And Dr. Boufford apologized for having to pay me less than what I ordinarily earned.

To add to all the other chaos, the Inspector General followed me around New York for two years, to see if I was billing for bogus services. Of course, he came up with nothing. Humorously, one of the tough guy investigators took me aside one day to ask whether I thought he ought to keep the beard he was growing! I look back and remember the stress of this media delirium. If I had only known then what I know now. The experience taught me to make lemonade from the sour lemons hurled at me.

Because of the expert job I had done, I received offers from hospitals around the country to do for their presidents what I had done for Dr. Boufford. That media mishap actually amplified my business, and put me on the map as a well-regarded nationally-known Relationship and Media Strategist and Coach. Who would have known?

Gilda-Gram®
When something happens TO us,
it really happens FOR us.

It's then up to us to determine what that FOR is, and pursue it. That may really be the hardest part of any media fiasco while it's occurring!

AMPLIFIER 46

EYE-ALOGUE, DYA-LOGUE, MONO-LOGUE

As ready as you are to deal with your audience, most audiences have a lot of things on their minds other than you. Because of their own stressors, listeners often face a speaker with a "Ho Hum . . ." attitude. Yes, we all suffer from information overload.

The able speaker will have completed and adhered to the **Audience Analysis Sheet**. Because he's done his homework, he knows the profiles and pitfalls of the audience before him. But knowing the listeners' proclivities alone is not enough. The speaker must get beyond the "Ho Hum . . ." block by incorporating an initial attention-getter that immediately touches the listeners' lives.

Many speakers believe their best attention-getting devices are their words and phrases. They reason that by saying the right thing right away, the listener will want to hear more. So, the average speaker immediately goes into a MONO-LOGUE, describing who he is and what he does, in an effort to sell himself upfront.

If it's only two people talking, eventually, the dyad of two conversationalists will engage in a DYA-LOGUE, where there is reciprocal back-and-forth jockeying of details. Through DYA-LOGUE, at least it seems that each party is giving the other an opportunity for a platform.

Finally, there is that real connection, that true exchange of feelings, witnessed in the eyes. I call that EYE-ALOGUE. And so, the usual scenario plays out in a 3-step progression of MONO-LOGUE, DYA-LOGUE, and EYE-ALOGUE.

BUT THAT'S NOT THE WAY TO PROJECT YOUR POWER. When MONO-LOGUE begins the process, DYA-LOGUE and EYE-ALOGUE often never occur, because the listener has dropped out long before that.

For a speaker to be understood, he must first show he is willing to understand the listener. How is he to do this quickly? Remember that the listener does not give the speaker much time before it's listener naptime.

<u>**Gilda-Gram®**</u>
**It's only 5 seconds before listeners
take their first mental vacation.**

So what can you do as a speaker? *It all begins in your eyes.* The eyes are the only part of our central nervous system that directly connect with another person. EYE-ALOGUE is empathic eye contact. We are visual beings. Our visual memory is 200 times greater than our verbal memory.

EYE-ALOGUE is conducted before any words are exchanged. The strength of its message communicates, "I care about your needs . . . and what you are about to say." It gracefully and gradually opens the door for more. And when you're doing a TV interview, your audience is watching your actions and reactions--especially those in your eyes!

EYE-ALOGUE is not the mere exchange of simple eye contact. Good eye communication means more than just a fleeting glance. When individuals communicate with one another, EYE-ALOGUE should last from 5 to 15 seconds.

When people communicate in groups, EYE-ALOGUE should last about 5 seconds as your eyes jump from person to person. EYE-ALOGUE whose duration is more than 15 seconds may be intimidating and/or too intimate for casual conversation. Yet, for the sake of communicating a sense of your involvement, where we would *like* 90% of our personal and business communications to be, EYE-ALOGUE of anything less than 5 seconds may connote the speaker isn't that interested. These rules generally apply only to the speaker, not to the listener.

Alicia is a minister of a small church. When she leads the worship service, she keeps her eyes closed for 2 or 3 seconds between glances at her parishioners. Her attempt is to don a Godly stance. But instead, she gives the impression of aloofness. This "slow blink" habit also carries into her personal conversations. Her listeners feel distance from her.

Barry is a film producer who habitually looks at the chin of his listeners. Without realizing it, he sends an impression of awkwardness and distance.

Mary is a human resources director for a large conglomerate. While she interviews people in her office, she often looks out her window as she asks questions. She appears disengaged. Interviewees routinely leave her office feeling angry that she wasted their time.

Pat is a professional speaker, exciting audiences with dramatic personal stories and anecdotes. However, she undermines her personal impact by looking at people in her audience for only half a second or less. Her audiences do not feel that she is talking to them.

All four people do not know how to project their power with the use of EYE-ALOGUE as I describe in Chapter 4 of "Don't

Bet on the Prince!" The language of EYE-ALOGUE is universal. People from different cultures and countries can express themselves and are understood solely through their eyes.

In a keynote speech I gave to international oil executives who spoke different languages from distant parts of the world, each was able to correctly identify the meanings behind the photos they were shown. There are only 4 emotions people can display: gladness, sadness, madness, and scaredness. The EYE-ALOGUE in the pictures was able to correctly communicate each of these 4 no matter what language the viewers spoke.

Eye-Alogue Exercise

Using your eyes alone, without words or facial expression, look in a mirror and:
1. Demonstrate gladness.
2. Demonstrate sadness.
3. Demonstrate madness.
4. Demonstrate scaredness.

Which felt most natural for you? Why? (There are no right answers; your response should only reflect your personality. What did you learn from this exercise?)

While developing my concept of EYE-ALOGUE, my research uncovered these facts:

1. In the United States, people from the east coast, the west coast, and major cities engage in more EYE-ALOGUE than others not within these regions. Apparently, cosmopolitan types are less intimidated by the invitation that EYE-ALOGUE offers.

2. Listeners engage in more EYE-ALOGUE than speakers. This is probably so that they can attend to what the speaker is saying; when their turn comes to take the floor, their part of the repartee will flow naturally because they have watched the speaker carefully.

3. In the United States, EYE-ALOGUE for short periods of time is appropriate; prolonged EYE-ALOGUE may be interpreted as romantic or intimidating.

4. Women establish more EYE-ALOGUE than men, probably because of their traditional subordination to males in society. Yet, women will avert their gaze quickly from men so as not to give sexual innuendoes.

5. Males discontinue EYE-ALOGUE with other males in our culture to ward off the suggestion of homosexuality.

After EYE-ALOGUE has set the stage for rapport and respect in a conversation, DYA-ALOGUE can work its magic. Drawing from the principles of Neuro Linguistic Programming, there are 2 steps:

Step #1
"Read" the EYE-ALOGUE of the speaker:
--"Visual" communicators look up before telling u they "see" our point of view.

--"Auditory" communicators look from side to side before explaining they won't "hear" our argument.

--"Kinesthetic" communicators look diagonally downward before admitting they "feel" we are right.

Step #2

Listen to the verbs the speaker uses. Are they visual, auditory, or kinesthetic? If the speaker is authentic, his verbs will match his EYE-ALOGUE.

When it's your turn to respond, deliberately match your DYA-LOGUE to the "see," "hear," or "feel" words the speaker had been using. For example:

--If the speaker looks up . . . and tells you that your idea "looks" good, you can DYA-LOGUE back with, "Let's 'see' if we can 'clear' up any of the 'oversights' of the plan tomorrow.

--If the speaker's eyes dart from side to side . . . and he indicates that he "hears" what you mean, DYA-LOGUE back by explaining what you "heard" the president "say."

--If the speaker looks diagonally downward . . . and lets you know that he "feels" you have a valid point, indicate you are "hopeful" that the company will "push" ahead with its plans.

The point here is to enhance interpersonal communication with speaker and listener on the same page. EYE-ALOGUE, followed by DYA-LOGUE, is the courting and prepping of our listener as we begin to establish rapport.

Since people do business with people they like, and since people like people like themselves, congruent communion is vital. DYA-LOGUE is powerful. It answers the needs of both communicators so each feels validated. Only in this way can win-win outcomes occur.

A speaker's MONO-LOGUE contains the only real reason he is communicating in the first place. How salespeople turn people off as they go through a rote MONO-LOGUE without considering the listener's needs. If only they knew their MONO-LOGUE should be preceded by EYE-ALOGUE and DYA-LOGUE!

If listening remains the passive sport of the couch potato, the speaker might as well not speak at all. The measure of successful interchange is the rapport between speaker and listener who are communicating in sync.

While sitting with four people to brainstorm how we could unify our talents, I observed one woman's EYE-ALOGUE dance back and forth to another woman. I noticed this dancing EYE-ALOGUE occurred after each of my suggestions about how we could divide the work. I read their EYE-ALOGUE as being negative towards my proposals.

Because of my perceptions, instead of offering more points for discussion, I altered my approach. I began to ask this woman questions about how she saw the fit of our talents. We DYA-LOGUED until she finally expressed her concerns. No longer could she and the other woman conceal their negativity.

As a result of my reading this EYE-ALOGUE for what it was, and subsequently pursuing my DYA-LOGUE differently, my MONO-LOGUE became a summation of what I believed we needed to do next. Time was saved and we all went off to individually explore the possibilities — which I knew would never come to fruition, based on my reading of this woman True to form, this group never met again.

But because of my "get things done" approach, another person at the table pulled me aside after the meeting and offered me a better proposal. His MONO-LOGUE style mirrored mine. He said he was impressed with the way I had picked up on the negative interplay of the two women, and how I jumped in to salvage our time. He and I continue to work together today.

Understand a speaker's style by reading his EYE-ALOGUE, then following up with the appropriate DYA-LOGUE and MONO-LOGUE. By DYA-LOGUING AND MONO-LOGUING in the language of the listener, rapport and trust can build — IF there is a possible bond.

Summary
To achieve rapport, apply
EYE-ALOGE, DYA-LOGUE, MONO-LOGUE
...in that order

AMPLIFIER 47

HOW TO HANDLE A HOSTILE AUDIENCE WITH EYE-ALOGUE

Turn conflict into common ground by using your strongest weapon — your eyes!

***

Adapted from an article written and presented by this author in UK for IEEE (Institute of Electrical and Electronics Engineers)

Public speaking is the Number 1 fear for most people. But if you're speaking in front of a hostile audience, fear is certainly to be expected. Nobody wants to be the recipient of a public persecution. Opposition and anger should be addressed as soon as possible. Otherwise, additional resentment builds, and with the slightest provocation, an entire auditorium can become unmanageable.

Many public speakers open their presentations with a prepared monologue — one that bridges the audience's agenda with their own. Others immediately immerse the audience in participative dialogue to build enthusiasm and activate involvement. But both monologue and dialogue heavily rely on words to get their meanings across. And because as little as 7 percent of our information is communicated through words alone, a speaker's best bet is to first communicate with facial and body expressions, particularly with his eyes.

Before uttering a single word, engage in an EYE-ALOGUE — prolonged empathic eye contact. More penetrable than MONO-LOGUE, and more disclosing that DYA-LOGUE, EYE-ALOGUE can help to establish rapport and cooperation — especially among hostile parties.

Secrets Behind EYE-ALOGUE

Former President Ronald Reagan used EYE-ALOGUE before he began each press conference. He looked reporters in the eyes — and then smiled and greeted them by name. This initial EYE-ALOGUE told his viewers, "I'm on your side." It promoted Reagan's reputation as "the great communicator."

Mikhail Gorbachev was considered by many to be one of the world's best speakers. Using his hands and voice as well, he first dominated a meeting with his eyes.

We focus much attention on our eyes with flattering eyeglass frames, tinted contact lenses, and colorful eye makeup. Our vocabulary substantiates the richness of EYE-ALOGUE: gaze, glance, glare, gawk, and gape are just a few synonyms for "look."

By noting the direction of a listener's glances during EYE-ALOGUE, a speaker can choose words that are derivatives of "see," "hear," or "feel" in an effort to connect with the eye cues before him. Based on the principle of Like Likes Like," this connecting of speaker's vocabulary to listener's EYE-ALOGUE enhances subliminal interpersonal communication, especially under hostile conditions.

The Speaker's Weapon

After your usual introduction, pause silently before the

angry group that sits before you. Divide the audience into imaginary quadrants, and for 3 seconds each, 12 seconds in all, seek out friendly eyes among the faces. Have an EYE-ALOGUE with each of these — and then smile.

Finally, take a breath and honestly acknowledge your listeners' fears: "By now the information of the XYZ report is out in the open. We will need more time to analyze the findings. Tonight, let's openly discuss our mutual concerns. I will be glad to fill you in on the facts we currently have."

By using EYE-ALOGUE to establish unity, you are setting the stage for believable DYA-LOGUE. With each question from the audience, you can now offer a sympathetic MONO-LOGUE in response. When you're finished, conduct EYE-ALOGUE for another few seconds, then smile to some friendly audience eyes.

Call upon a receptive face for Question #1. With subsequent queries, when possible, note the interrogator's eyes and respond in visual, auditory, or kinesthetic terms: "I see what you are saying" (for a visual interrogator), "I can hear how upset you are" (for an auditory interrogator), and "I understand why you feel as you do" (for a kinesthetic interrogator). If a hostile interrogator gets carried away, quickly disengage eye contact with him, and engage in EYE-ALOGUE with friendlier audience members.

When used properly, EYE-ALOGUE can be the prefect prelude to a DYA-LOGUE and MONO-LOGUE that contains your real agenda. Note that this formula inverts the usual tendency of speakers to begin with their prepared agenda and to MONO-LOGUE an audience to sleep. This is your best shot at allaying audience resistance and achieving your objectives.

AMPLIFIER 48

YOUR VOICE OF CHOICE

The vocal impact we make on others consists of the rate at which we speak, our pitch, our rhythm, our volume, and our use of pauses. (Yes, there is power in pausing!) Our vocal tones account for 38% of the impression we make when we are face-to-face with a listener, and 78% of our impact when we are on the telephone or any audio device.

According to a 20-year study of 300 alumni of Stanford's Graduate School of Business, a person's verbal skills is the single most important factor that affects her career success. Energetic, enthusiastic, outgoing personalities with polished speaking skills earn higher salaries than sweet talkers or proverbial "nice guys." Voice is an aspect of our self-identity. It mirrors our self-image.

We use our voice to communicate who we are and what we think. Simply, a negative voice interferes with our communication. At least 50% of Americans have aesthetically disturbing voices or actual vocal problems due to the misuse or abuse of the vocal mechanism. Ten to 25% of these people could develop chronic voice conditions such as nodes, polyps, and other growths on the vocal folds, such as premalignant tumors. Most people don't realize that proper voice control can be a serious health concern.

The first part of the listening process involves sensing someone's sound waves. If the sounds we hear are "pleasant," our interpretation and evaluation of the meaning of the information he is communicating will be more accepted.

"Pleasant" generally relates to the *like likes like* factor: listeners like speakers who sound like themselves. Because of this, I often counsel New Yorkers who sound "too Noo Yawk" to modify their speech sounds when presenting to people in other parts of the country. This *like likes like* factor determines the way a listener responds--without his being aware of it.

How Listeners Process Information
1. Hear
2. Interpret
3. Evaluate
4. Respond

Jerry came to see me to rid his Brooklyn accent. It seemed that he was being discriminated against on the telephone throughout the country before he met prospective customers. I pointed to his nasality, a common problem when someone talks through his nose. In general, nasal sounds depict complaining, disagreeable characters. Voices that resonate from the chest are considered more personable and persuasive.

Some nasality is necessary, but only for the sounds "n," "m," and "ng." I asked Jerry to pinch his nose closed and say, "They ran fourteen miles, falling and stumbling near the finish." Then, "She sang seventeen songs and swooned." He noted his nasal vibrations with the letters "n," "m," and "ng." I asked him to hold his nose again and say, "Woe, oh horse of mine." The only buzzing in his nose came from the word "mine." We audiotaped his responses so that Jerry, himself, could hear his projection.

When Jerry recognized his nasality, I asked him to open his mouth more to emit his vowel sounds. As soon we he was able to modify his speech, he noticed that his business increased. Again, we raise the issue: Is this manipulation or speaking in the voice of the receiver so that you can better be heard? Only you need be comfortable with your response. The differences in vocal sounds between men and women serve to stereotype our power. The first President Bush's voice was ridiculed as being too high-pitched, a trait considered to be unforgivable for a male in our culture. Men are "supposed" to have deep, masculine voice tones. After he was "media-trained" and taught to draw from his lower pitch, Bush's voice became appealing enough for him to be elected.

Former President Ronald Reagan's voice was considered to be an asset. Although it was not the voice of an orator, it was low-pitched, husky, sometimes fading to a whisper, and extraordinarily intimate. As the adage goes, it is not so much what you say but how you say it. Each one of us has a unique vocal quality that we can project to define our power. Reagan's certainly was distinctive.

In presidential races that followed, questions arose as to whether the voice as well as the style of each candidate sounded "presidential enough." For any person, a whispering voice might be interpreted as belonging to someone who is weary, depressed, or meek. To determine if you are a whisperer, put a finger against your Adam's apple and say "Zzzzz." There should be a vibration. In contrast, do the same thing, but this time with the sound "Sssss." Your larynx will not vibrate with the latter sound because this is an unvoiced whisper, whereas "Zzzzz" is not.

Whisper speaking should not be confused with soft speaking. Projecting a Power Image requires a wide range of infinite gradations of volume from very quiet to very strong.

One of my graduate students spoke with a voice so high-pitched that a listener would think she was putting it on in an effort to be "cute." Part of the course required students to make class presentations. When she finished hers, she consulted with me after class. She confided that she was seeing a speech therapist to lower her pitch. I asked her to tell
me about her childhood. She said that she was the youngest child of 4 older brothers. I asked if her being the youngest girl, a "doll" to her brothers, might have had anything to do with the voice she had learned to project.

She indicated that that issue had come up with the therapist. It raises the issue of how much of our voice is due to nature or to nurture. For years, scientists have argued the nature vs. nurture controversy. Only you can think about how your upbringing has prepared you for the voice you are taking on unconsciously.

Many women are criticized for having not only voices that are high-pitched and piercing, but for also being too emotional. Women must refrain from whining, which is negatively perceived as a "female" trait. They should also avoid over-smiling, which projects the vocal tones into high-end grating octaves. Yes, the more we smile during our speaking, the more positively we are received. However, women must be careful they don't overdo the smiling, so it's a fine line to walk between smiling and smiling too much.

Similarly, no speaker wants to sound monotone. The average voice runs a scale of 12 to 20 notes. Monotones may use only 5 notes in their conversation. If those 5 notes are at a highly piercing octave, that may be especially unnerving to a listener. I recently watched a movie starring a gorgeous young woman.

As beautiful as she was, her voice was so high-pitched, I couldn't continue watching her performance. She seemed like a little girl, and she became unbelievable to me in her character's role. I was actually surprised the casting director either chose her for the part, or directed her in this piercing direction.

The sound of emotionalism for women is often a result of the use of high-low glides. Barbara routinely whined "Oh (ascending), how (descending) awful (ascending, then descending)." Her male colleagues criticized her behind her back for being over-emotional. She was passed over when it came for her to be promoted. When Barbara demanded an explanation, she was simply told, "We don't think you can be a powerful leader in our company." Emotionalism and power are not viewed as a compatible combination.

Whenever any person becomes emotional, his voice naturally rises. Because women have wider vocal ranges than men, they are often accused of being too emotional when their voices reach higher octaves. (Which really comes first: the emotionalism or the vocal pitch?) It is easier for males in our culture to take on angry voices; their higher pitches do not invite the same negative connotations as do women's piercing sounds.

Studies show that people who feel more composed are perceived as more powerful. Perhaps this is due to the interpretation by most that a low-pitched voice represents a person who is in command. Perhaps that is because low-pitched voices are masculine. A lower pitch and its accompanying image of composure can be developed as a result of proper breath control.

It's horrifying that 1 in 3 Americans now contracts some form of cancer. The exception to this horrifying statistic is found among athletes, where only 1 in 7 contracts the disease. One researcher discovered that he could actually create malignant growths by decreasing the amount of oxygen in a person's system. Deep breathing enhances the oxygen supply in the cells. A study of 20 opera singers by the National Institute on Aging and the University of Maryland, found that singers live longer because they breathe better. By constantly using their diaphragm, they condition their heart and lungs. Athletes, like opera singers, must develop strengthened breath control.

I coached Sol to develop his presentation skills. Amazingly, he found that his endurance for his hobby of deep sea diving improved drastically as a result of the exercises we did with his diaphragm. In a similar vein, the New York City newspapers reported that a professional dancer who had been stabbed repeatedly in the heart by a mugger LIVED due to her physical fitness.

Deep breathing controls the flow of lymph fluid necessary to cleanse the human system with white blood cells. Unlike the heart that pumps blood throughout the body, the lymph system, without such a pump, depends upon deep diaphragmatic breathing to accomplish its cleansing process. Yoga practitioners can accelerate lymph cleansing by 15 times the normal pace when they incorporate deep diaphragmatic breathing. This process broadens and deepens a person's vocal tones so that he sounds as though he is in command of his power.

Deep breathing provides additional rewards. It gives a person two sources or cavities of air--the stomach and the chest--instead of just one. It takes pressure off the shoulder area, which reduces throat strain and neck tension and which creates unpleasant voice sounds. It requires less work than high chest breathing because of the diaphragm's cone shape which can be raised and lowered easily to change volume, quality, and rate of speech.

Pandemic Aside, Use Your Mask

Visualize the surgical masks worn during the pandemic. They fit beneath the eyes to cover the nose and mouth. To eliminate poor vocal sounds produced through the lower throat, or larynx, produce your speech through the mask area (the nose and mouth). Mask voice production opens your voice, improves its range, gives it warmth and richness, fills it with expression, and projects your vocal power.

Increase Your Breath Capacity

Healthy vocal cords should be able to hold the sound "ah" for 25 seconds. To develop the capacity of your diaphragm, place one hand on your chest, the other on your diaphragm. Breathe in at a ratio of 7 to 1. Inhale through your nose for 7 counts. Hold your breath for 1 count. Exhale through your mouth for 7 counts. Move only the diaphragm, not the chest.

To confirm that you're breathing from the diaphragm, place your hands on your abdomen, fingers pointing together. As you inhale, push *out* against your hands with your lower ribs and abdomen. As you exhale through your mouth, your abdomen should *pull in*.

By the same token, as you talk, your stomach should move in, smoothly and gradually. You will know that you are not breathing properly if your upper chest and shoulders heave up and down when you speak. This misuse of your diaphragm creates tension and strain in your throat, interferes with your volume, and is generally both mentally and physically exhausting.

I was participating in a Peloton cycling class with an instructor wearing a midriff top, allowing us to see how perfectly she used her diaphragm. Her chest and neck were devoid of movement, as her breathing and speaking strongly pumped air in and out of her diaphragm. Since her top exposed her bare abdomen, her use of diaphragmatic breathing was evident. With her application of correct breath control, I knew the class was being taught by a true athlete.

It is the proper use of your diaphragm that releases the tension from your larynx. It is the diaphragm that controls the
largest amount of oxygen you can get. It is the diaphragm that projects your power sound. Since your power cannot be emitted through consonants, concentrate especially on pumping out your five vowels: "a," "e," "i," "o" and "u."

Proper breath control also modulates a person's pitch. An appropriate power voice will avoid problems caused by unnecessary strain on the vocal cords. Some of these problems may begin as a sore or hoarse throat, develop into nodes or nodules, and evolve into throat cancer. I tell clients who speak a lot on their jobs to do vocal exercises to relax and retrain the voice. The following are especially recommended:

--Drop your head to your chest and roll it alternatingly to the right, then to the left, nearly touching each ear to each shoulder. Repeat the process slowly several times.

--Sigh deeply, letting your whole body slump to the ground.

--Pant like a puppy on a hot day, with mouth open and tongue hanging out. This will open your air canal and build strength in your diaphragm.

--Open your jaw and slowly say "ah." Yawn deeply to open your throat, to force rich oxygen into your diaphragm, and to relax your neck, throat, and tongue.

--Inhale and exhale slowly and deeply using the 7 to 1 breathing ratio.

Note how all these exercises lower your pitch.

Despite the fact that Joseph was president of a prestigious company, his feelings of inner powerlessness were transparent when he conversed. At cocktail parties, when asked what he did for a living, he cleared his throat once . . . then cleared it again . . . and then again--before responding, "Uh, I'm President of . . . uh . . . Allied Corp."

When a voice is misused, nature protects and soothes the vocal cords by releasing a flow of mucus over the vocal fold. The throat then needs to be cleared of this mucus in order for
speech to be clear. Continued voice abuse persists in squeezing the voice box. The gland under the vocal fold releases more mucus and again, the throat needs to be cleared.
The cycle is perpetuated until only coughing succeeds in clearing the mucus. This, in turn, further irritates the vocal mechanism. The voice grows tired and hoarse.

The misuse of the vocal mechanism can be a reflection of the stress in one's life. As we worked on his inner power, I discovered that Joseph really did not feel comfortable in his position. When people had asked him about his job, his insecurity about the position he held made his vocal cords tense. He damagingly forced the sound through his larynx which created mucus that he had to clear before he could speak clearly.

A few weeks later, his company declared bankruptcy. By careful observation, a listener could tell that the man was already emotionally bankrupt before his company announced the news. A Power Image comes from within.

Most people take their voices for granted and abuse their vocal cords. Margie, an author about to go on a nation-wide book tour to promote her book, came to work with me with a very hoarse voice. Unknowledgeable and unassertive about her right to request a microphone for her speaking engagements, she had been literally screaming in front of audiences for a long time. To many listeners, stridency and shrillness are often more disagreeable than nasality.
I told Margie that her neck looked taut. She looked at me in disbelief. I pointed to how her veins and cords stood out. I showed her how the muscles around her chin were tight. I tied a ribbon snugly around her neck. She watched the ribbon begin to choke her as she ended each sentence.

Margie was shaken about the possibility of losing her voice completely. Her sound was so raspy that I suggested she see medical doctor who specialized in the ear, nose, and throat. She insisted that she did not need to do that; in fact, her father was a surgeon with that very specialty! I told her that I would assign some exercises that she could do. But I really felt she needed immediate care from a physician. She left, unhappy.

Weeks later she called me. She had, indeed, totally lost her voice. Conceding that I might be correct, she finally made a trip to her father's office. Not only did she require surgery on her vocal cords, but he also prescribed the same vocal exercises that I had assigned his daughter. Use your voice correctly in advance to prevent such problems later.

No communications professional can tell you what your proper pitch should be. Each of us must individually find it for ourselves. To find your proper pitch, try this exercise:

>--Raise your arms above your head.

>--With lips closed, say, "Um, hum, one; Um, hum, two; Um, hum, three . . . Um, hum, four, . . . all the way to ten."

>--Check that your pitch of the number is at the same level as your "Um, hum."

>--Check that your nose and lips are humming and resonating.

>--The sound of those "Um, hum's" is your proper pitch.

>--With that pitch, say, "Good morning."

>--Say, "My name is . . ."

Now, with the same pitch, repeat the following energy words which naturally bring the voice forward to the mask area:

>--Hello
>--Really
>--Beautiful
>--Right
>--Ready
>--No

--Go
--Do

You might feel dizzy at first after performing these exercises. This is a temporary condition caused by excessive oxygen intake. The dizziness will pass quickly.

I have trained whole audiences, quickly and easily, to find and use their proper pitch. Not only does proper pitch save the voice, it also projects your power.

Powerful people speak slowly, as though time were plentiful. Each word is enunciated. Each thought is completed before new information is introduced. At the point of pause, the voice naturally drops. Powerful people use pauses that command their listeners to wait until they are ready to complete their thoughts.

Power is patience. If there were ever a clue to someone who feels inwardly powerless, it is the person whose patience runs thin. Tony usually drove quickly and recklessly, leaning heavily on the car's horn. John often becomes impatient and angry when people in front of him on the crowded city sidewalks walk too slowly.

Both are quick to raise their vocal volume and pitch to a loud scream. Both communicate emotions that are out of control. Both need to discover their true internal power buried deep within.

What to Expect During Voice Re-training

1. Your voice may appear to have a sing-song quality. This is part of your new versatility and vocal power.

2. Some physical changes may include:
    --soreness along your neck
    --tickling in and around your ear
    --burning in your soft palate

These conditions result from realignment of your throat muscles as pressure lift from your voice box and moves up to your jaw. It is similar to muscular soreness experienced by beginning athletes. It will disappear in no more than a few weeks.

3. You may develop a trimmer midriff as your midsection muscles are toned and firmed.

4. The bones in your head prevent you from hearing your new voice as others do. Your voice may appear to you to be louder than it really is. Even your voice played back to you on a tape recorder is only a *sense* of what others hear because distortion is created according to our perceptions.

5. Like every learning experience, your initial progress will plateau or even regress at times. Your breath control may become frustrating. Don't give up. All learning takes time and patience while it follows the natural learning curve.

Take the Audio Test

Although not a perfect reflection of how our voice really sounds to other people, the tape recorder is the best device we have. Follow this regimen:

--Record your voice on audiotape 3 times for 2 minutes each, once in the morning, once in the afternoon, and once in the evening. For example, your morning recording can consist of your reading the newspaper aloud. Your evening recording can consist of your reading the street signs aloud as you drive home from work.

--Are the 3 recordings of your voice the same or different?

--When do you find your pitch to be most powerful? least powerful?

--Look for vocal diversity in every one of your voice recordings.

--Monitor your breath support while you are recording by occasionally placing one hand on your midsection when you speak. Does your stomach move OUT as you speak and IN as you breathe?

--LAUGH. Laughter is a natural reflection of your optimal pitch.

--Measure your audio voice according to the following characteristics that make for either a powerless or a powerful voice:

The PowerLESS Voice
--monotone
--raises voice at end of a statement, as though it is a question
--begins sentences clearly, but fizzles out the end words
--small, barely audible
--loud, blaring
--accusing tone
--really-doesn't-matter-tone
--whiny

--uses unempowered words such as : "Ummmm," "You know," "OK?," "Right," "Like," "Sort of," "Kind of," "Well, ah . . ."
--giggles
--nervous laugh
--frequent throat-clearing
--begins but does not finish sentences

The POWERFUL Voice
--well-modulated, adding different tones for emphasis
--makes direct statements, bringing them to clear, concise endings
--firm, positive tone
--flowing presentation of information
--no extraneous words or sounds

The payoffs of projecting your vocal power are far-reaching. A power voice enhances your interpersonal communications, as well as your business success. When a person incorporates vocal power, he can turn a hearer into an active and involved listener. As we know, this will encourage a long-lasting relationship.

AMPLIFIER 49

WORDS THAT COUNT

One survey found that the consequences people fear most about speaking in public include making embarrassing mistakes, damaging their career or reputation, forgetting, freezing or finding themselves unable to speak, being dull or boring, and looking nervous or petrified. These fears are encouraged by sayings like, "The human brain starts working the moment you are born and never stops until you stand up to speak in public."

No doubt, listeners equate your language with your intelligence. Communications guru, Don Bagin, reminds us that a person can go through life not knowing the authors of classics, not knowing where Argentina is on the map, and not knowing how to figure a square root. He says chances are that no one will even notice these deficiencies. But when it comes to talking--you just can't fake it. Listeners are quick to place a poor speaker into a "verbal ghetto" and stereotype him in a negative way.

Cocktail party small talk (public speaking in miniature) raises as much blood pressure as speaking in a larger arena. So, you can imagine what a media interview can do. Without a glass in one hand and a pocket (or a cigarette or an hors d'oeuvre) in the other, people often express their discomfort not only at how to maneuver their limbs, but also at what to mutter.

Yes, speaking in public might be terrifying. Most people are unsure of their MONO-LOGUE. Yet, Americans use only about 500 words in 20 to 30 different ways. Why is assembling the right words such a problem?

Typically, when clients seek me out for media coaching, they sport pages of notes, showing thousands of words and hours of preparation on what they want to get across. They are shocked when I tell them that the words they use only account for 7% of the impact they make. Imagine the time wasted constructing *words* that could better be invested on enhancing body language (55%) and voice projection (38%)!

Even when our words are being attended to, as explained earlier, only 25% of our message will be processed, with just 10% remembered. This supports the popular proverb, "I hear, I forget; I see, I remember; I do, I understand." *Seeing* information can increase remembering to 25%. *Doing an exercise* can instill 90% of its meaning in our brain. That surely confirms that people hear--only to forget. As the writer Norman Cousins said, "The more you say, the less people remember." That should surely sober you up as you prepare for any media interview.

Because a person can listen at about twice the speed he can speak, the listener's mind wanders. A study of college students found that only 12% of the audience listened to the information imparted during a particular lecture; the rest attended to things as diverse as daydreaming and sexual fantasies.

A group of 140 managers and consultants were polled for tricks they use to stay awake during boring business speeches. Some 61% write notes, 47% daydream, 41% doodle, 19% ask questions, 19% read, and 11% talk to a neighbor. Many employed several of these tricks. Yet, 18% still said they fall asleep.

We spend 80% of our waking hours communicating. Probably more than half that time is spent *listening*. Yet, the average school curriculum teaches writing for 12 years, reading for 6 to 8 years, speaking for 1 to 2 years, and listening for 0 to 1/2 year! We are finally becoming aware of this deficiency in business as company time and money are lost because of messages that either did not get transmitted correctly, or did not get out at all.

The quality of listening we use in our families is no better. Years ago, it was found that the average person interacts only *12 minutes per day* with his spouse, yet watches *many hours* of television. The average father spends *12 minutes per week* interacting with each of his children, and of those, *8.5 minutes* are spent arguing about television, food habits, and homework. Princeton University found that pre-pandemic, the average *quality* time that one parent spends with his or her child is no more than *5 minutes per day*. That included listening, laughing, and playing, rather than ordering, complaining, or demanding.

It is no wonder that children--as well as mates--complain that their parents and partners don't listen. And it's not a surprise that during the pandemic of 2020, families were freaking out because they suddenly were thrust into stay-at-home situations. Many hardly recognized their mates, and they didn't even know their kids' preferences about eating, sleeping, learning, and friends.

Especially during the pandemic, TV viewing bounced back to America's Number 1 non-work activity. Thanks to our televisions, along with our techie equipment, our attention spans have become shorter and shorter. Many years ago, with the advent of the remote control, a study found that we change channels every 3 minutes, 42 seconds. (How many of us today actually wait a full 3 minutes until we zap the remote? Few, I would think!)

We are programmed to attend for not more than 30 seconds at a time to any media message, because we've been trained so well by our commercials. Even when L'Eggs did a radio commercial featuring *me* as one of their "Women on the Move," the 45-second pitch felt too long even for me to hear a commercial about myself!

The average length of time allotted by TV news for an interview, the soundbite, *used to be* 45 seconds. Now it has been lowered from 30 seconds to 9 seconds in some cases. People seem to want their information immediately, similar to their other gratifications. Recently, as spokesperson on national TV for a brand, I noticed that our soundbite on that evening's news was a full 18 seconds.

Because of its unusual length beyond the new 9-second norm, I knew the network intended to blow the topic into a major controversy. I was right. Days of follow-up stories on the topic continued; fortunately, we were prepared for the coverage because I had had the good sense of timing our media interview. Television viewers are programmed to endure for shorter periods of time and to develop increasingly poorer listening habits.

Add to the problem the differences in the way the genders tune in and out: Women often prefer emotion-laden terms ("feelings about the job," "caring about subordinates," "upset about his promotion"); many men relate better to sports metaphors ("winning and losing," "going down to the wire," "hitting paydirt"). Further, women talk *details* while men talk *deals*.

We also learn that when men and women speak, 96% of the interruptions come from men. If there is a war between the sexes, women learn that when it comes to their communication with men, they can forget the old adage that power corrupts; they learn quickly, instead, that power *interrupts*!

Does anyone listen anymore? If nobody hears our words, why speak at all? The answer is that words provide our framework, our excuse for conversation, our raison d'etre in the first place. The solution to our listening problems is to inject our first **5 seconds** with the most effective words we can find. That means, avoid 4 pitfalls of powerlessness: fillers, qualifiers, tag questions, and modifiers.

Pitfall # 1: FILLERS

How do you adjust to silent pauses in media conversations on air? Powerful people use pauses to their advantage. In fact, one way listeners distinguish between polished and unpolished speakers is by the length and duration of their pauses. By pausing, we gain and control our listeners' attention.

Powerless people *fill* their pauses with "well," "uh," "er," "ah," "umm." Former New York City Mayor Ed Koch was a master filler. Instead of his well-known "uh's," he could have used the almighty pause to color his speeches with emphasis and drama. His use of pauses would have increased the listening capacity of his audiences--and perhaps his popularity at the end of his reign. To eliminate fillers from one's speech, a person should keep his mouth closed until he decides exactly what he wants to say.

I was developing Lucy's empowerment skills with her. She admitted feeling uncomfortable with pauses in her conversations. One morning, she called her aggressive boss to say she would have to go cross-country to attend the funeral of her father. PAUSE. With Lucy's discomfort, she filled the pause with a very insecure, "Is that OK?" The boss began to scream at Lucy, no doubt, because he felt he could bully her. At once, the woman learned not to fill another pause in any of her conversations. Ever!

Pitfall # 2: QUALIFIERS

Qualifiers set the speaker up to fail. They confuse the listener by suggesting that the speaker may have a view different from that of the person he is speaking to. Sentences often begin with:
> "I'm sure you don't agree with this, but . . ."
> "It may not be your feeling, however . . ."
> "I'm not sure this is the case, but . . ."
> "I'm sorry to interrupt you, yet . . ."

As a result of confusing qualifiers, the listener must choose whether to defend his feelings about the first part of the speaker's statement ("Yes, I do agree with you, AND . . .") or to respond to the second portion ("I think the price of tea has become too high.")

Many people can only process one thought at a time. If an assertive statement were to follow the beginning disclaimer, it would take a perceptive and tenacious listener to discover it. Based on what we know about listening ability in general, such a possibility is unlikely.

Carol's continual beginning of each sentence with, "I'm sorry, but . . ." frustrated her boss so much that he promoted someone else to the position that should rightfully have gone to Carol. The boss stereotyped his subordinate as "too submissive" and "incapable of handling a more responsible job." Words DO matter!

Pitfall # 3: TAG QUESTIONS

Tag Questions convey that the speaker is reluctant to take a firm stand on an issue. Sentences are typically constructed with:

"I'm on Mulberry St., *aren't I?*"
"You didn't want to see that movie, *did you?*"
"Tom is a good boss, *don't you agree?*"

Tag Questions end with an upward vocal inflection, a questioning tone, that immediately discloses the insecurity of the speaker. Instead of employing Tag Questions in your discussions, ask questions as questions, and make statements with firm conviction. Questions and statements should stand independently of one another.

When Errol switched his use of Tag Questions to definitive, assertive declarations, his subordinates responded to him with greater respect and follow-through. Although no one could pinpoint the reason, Errol's image suddenly improved.

Pitfall #4: MODIFIERS

Modifiers remove the power from otherwise persuasive language. Some examples of modifying expressions and words are:

"perhaps"
"I think"
"maybe"
"it seems"
"you know"
"like"
"kind of"
"sort of"
"very"

"definitely"
"surely"

If a statement needs to add such modifiers, either the words cannot stand alone or the speaker feels insecure about using them. Whatever the case may be, the listener hears and interprets powerlessness.

Chris and I taped her speech patterns the first hour we worked together. She instantly recognized the modifiers; they were habitual. As she continues to be aware of them, and remove them from her vocabulary, friends are beginning to tell her how "assertive" she has suddenly become. (I wonder why! Wink!!)

If we get past the first 5 seconds to the 15-second mark of evaluation, we might have a shot for the 30-second stretch. At that point, before your listener is ready to switch channels, your projected power must be obvious enough to entice him to stay tuned for more.

The trick in getting beyond the 5-second mark is to use words that are unquestionably power*ful*. A study at Yale University named 12 power words:
>"money,"
>"new"
>"proven"
>"results"
>"save"
>"discover"
>"ease"
>"guarantee"
>"health"
>"love"
>"safety"
>"YOU."

To that list, I would also add the use of your listener's NAME. Including these power words in our MONOLOGUES is a start to using powerful language.

Similarly, a tech company listed the top power words salespeople should put into their advertising emails:
"now"
"you/your"
"Thanks"
"new"
"easy"
"and"
"free"
"your name"

Familiarizing yourself in advance with your audience will guide you to the list of power words that best fits your needs.

Your power expressions must project the image of a person who is not swayed by external mishaps and disappointments. That means no complaining or blaming! A few of the power*less* expressions I have gathered include:
"I can't"
"I should"
"It's not my fault"
"It's a problem"
"Life's a struggle"
"I hope"
"If only"
"It's terrible"
"I'll try."

Compare these with their alternatives:
"I won't"
"I could"

> "I'm totally responsible."
> "It's an opportunity."
> "Life's an adventure."
> "I know."
> "Next time."
> "It's a learning experience."
> "I'll do…"

The first group of words represents a philosophy of the proverbial glass half empty. The second represents the glass half full. Would you prefer to associate with someone whose glass is half of *anything*--or one whose cup runneth over?

Gilda-Gram®
The way you present your goblet determines how others will fill it.

Power words and expressions must also be constructed properly. Most people can't grasp the meaning behind a spoken sentence of more than 10 to 15 words, or one that includes more than 2 numbers. Therefore, use the bite-size approach to speaking. Speak cogently, clearly, and, above all, concisely. Occasionally count the number of words per sentence you use. You'll see if you are remaining on target.

Brevity also pertains to the size of the words you choose. Whereas short people in our society may be discriminated against, short words are usually praised. Note how pithy and pointed the following sentences sound:

> "For sale."
> "I'm through."
> "Don't smoke."
> "It's a deal."
> "I love you."

In these simple sentences, each word with only one syllable requires no questions about its meaning.

By empowering your MONO-LOGUE with words that count, the paltry 7% of our projected image--our words--will have a better chance to relay significant meaning. More importantly, your message will have a better chance of being heard and recalled. Powerful people are remembered and referred. That is the major ingredient for building rapport.

AMPLIFIER 50

AVOID TECHNICAL JARGON

Listeners get lost in technical terms.

Can you translate the meaning of these 2 sentences?

1. Scintillate, scintillate, asteroid minific.

2. It is fruitless to become lachrymose over precipitately departed lacteal fluid.

I often train technical people who use a language all their own. To alert them to their own technical jargon, I assign them the difficult task of explaining to an 8-year-old what they do for a living. There's a lot of laughter in the room as they recognize how stumped they often are!

The best public speakers are able to charm an audience by adapting to the listeners' level of understanding. Before you launch a new presentation, always return to your **Audience Analysis Shee**t to assess who your listeners are.

It's your turn now. Explain to an 8-year-old what you do for a living. Write what you would say.

How difficult was that for you? Why?

AMPLIFIER 51

PART 8--FINALE
Know More than
Your Pre-Rehearsed Content

Introducing a new concept with terminology your audience has not heard before can turn into a dry discussion. However, during this segment, my quick-witted interviewer fed me great material for a lively repartee. I had no intention of introducing my EDM Technique. But the topic lent itself so well to it, I quickly pulled from my expertise. Watch "Dr. Gilda's EDM Flirting Technique,"
https://www.youtube.com/watch?v=sBGTMYJMD-w

During the hundreds of interviews I've done, it has happened often that the interviewer goes in another direction from the one planned. A guest needs to be quick-thinking to travel wherever the host takes her.

You've studied my EYE-ALOGUE/DYA-LOGUE/MONO-LOGUE Technique in PART 6 of this program. For this segment, because this interview was veering in a different direction than planned, I re-named the concept "EDM." This TV audience had never heard my acronym. But the lively interchange I had with the host attracted many great comments on my social media.

It's easy to criticize a TV show from your comfy couch at home, and this is what the viewing public always does. So, develop a thick skin, project your best self, and have a good time.

Yes, every show has its issues. When I saw the playback of this one, I noticed the slide with my Gilda-Grams® had a misspelling of a word. Don't sweat this stuff. Guests are at a program's mercy, so accept that perfection is a myth.

My EDM Technique had apparently impressed the host; a few days later, she texted me to review what each letter stood for. Further interest is a sure way to be invited back!

1. This interview ran longer than most, for 5 minutes, 31 seconds. Did it keep your interest? Why or why not?

2. What will you remember about this segment?

3. What would you have liked to see me change?

4. What would you do differently if you were on screen?

PART 9
FINE TUNING YOUR MESSAGE

AMPLIFIER 52

WILL YOUR SOUNDBITES KEEP YOUR AUDIENCE AWAKE?

The best soundbites express emotions, instead of just stating facts. Sure, facts are relevant for professional reports, but emotion carries feelings for presentation. If a soundbite doesn't add emotion, determine whether you need it. See the difference in the following examples.

Weak
Police Officer: "The driver of the Toyota lost control, crossed the barrier, and hit the SUV traveling in the opposite direction."

Better
Police Officer: "It was one of the saddest crashes I ever saw. A mom, dad, and their three kids were killed."

Weak
School Principal: "The budget cuts will force us to cancel the school's art program."

Better
School Principal: "I feel terrible for the artistic kids in this school. When I told the Art Club we needed to close their program, a few of the budding artists started to cry."

Weak
Mayor: "I've earmarked an extra $3M to the Water Department budget to prevent water main breaks."

Better

Mayor: "I've personally been affected by the water main breaks! Last week, I lost water at my house, making it impossible for us to cook and do our laundry!"

Elicit Emotional Responses

Facts are easy to state, and are appropriate for written reports. These reports have the specific purpose of eliminating bias. But presentations and interviews must convey emotion to make their impact. That's what the soundbite does. Note how news reporters open their stories to grab viewers' attention by eliciting emotion. Yet it is one of the most overused tools.

Don't use a soundbite unless its drama will reel in your audience. Let your soundbites take your viewers with you to the scene. Boost your descriptions with dramatic soundbites that your audience can visualize as though they were there.

AMPLIFIER 53

POSITIVE BODY LANGUAGE CHECKLIST

1. Sit high in chair, with shoulders back, leaning slightly toward the interviewer

2. Uncross your arms in an open and receptive posture

3. Relax your hands, without fists

4. Open your facial expression, unobstructed by hands

5. Center your body and head, and look into the interviewer's eyes when you respond

6. Don't swivel in your chair

7. Cross your legs or leave them casually open

8. Don't stroke your chin or preen while on camera

9. Keep your eyes open, alert, and engaged

10. Mirror your interviewer's body positions and expressions

AMPLIFIER 54

EMPOWERMENT CHECKLIST

1. Remember that audiences receive information according to the Like Likes Like Dynamic.

2. Play to how your audience listens, by including visual, auditory, AND kinesthetic cues.

3. Communicate with EYE-ALOGUE, DYA-LOGUE, and MONO-LOGUE--in that order.

4. Hone your body language so that it "says" what you want it to say.

5. Hone your voice so it complements your body language.

6. Hone your words so they support the messages your body language and voice send.

7. Build rapport so your relationships can continue beyond showtime.

AMPLIFIER 55

NON-VERBAL MESSAGE CHECKLIST

It's not WHAT you say, it's the WAY you say it.

BODY EXPRESSION

PowerLESS
Rounded shoulders
Head down
Eyes downcast
Tightly-clasped hands
Slow, shuffle-type walk
Lack of hand gestures
Fiddling with hair, face, pencil
Sticking fingers in mouth

POWERFUL
Straight shoulders
Head erect
Relaxed arms & hands
Straight posture
Use of hand gestures
Responsive nod of head

FACIAL EXPRESSION

PowerLESS
Wandering eye movements
Stiff lips
Infrequent smiles
Staring into space
Stone face
Worried face
Tight-lipped smile

Covering mouth with hand
Biting cheek or lip
Excessive licking of lips
Excessive tongue movements

POWERFUL
Ready smile
Looking directly at interviewer while conversing
Smiling while speaking
Relaxed face and mouth

VOCAL EXPRESSION

PowerLESS
Speaking in monotone
Raising voice at the end of a sentence
Beginning sentences clearly, but fizzling out end words
Small, barely audible voice
Loud, blaring vice
Accusing tone
Using a "it-really-doesn't-matter" tone
Whining
Giggling
Ummmm," "You know," "like." "sort of," "kind of"
Nervous laugh
Frequent throat-clearing
Starting, but not finishing, sentences

POWERFUL
Well-modulated voice, adding different tones for emphasis
Making direct statements
Making direct statements, with clear, concise endings
Firm, positive tone
Flowing presentation
No extraneous words or sounds

AMPLIFIER 56

THE POWER OF BUILDING RAPPORT

Successful salespeople recognize that to increase their revenues, they must build and nurture rapport with their buyers. We are all salespeople. Whether it's a product, a service, a book, or an idea, the sale also always includes the way we sell ourselves. In business, it usually takes at least 5 interactions before a sale is closed, and usually more. Sometimes family members need even greater persuasion.

All in all, the higher the stakes, the more contacts and steps are needed. The challenge is to evolve distinctive relationships that exude depth and quality in a fast-paced world that rarely stands still long enough for such listening to occur.

Discussing Relationship Wellness topics, I was appearing on national and international TV several times a day each week for months. People didn't start recognizing me on the streets for perhaps 7 months after I started appearing. It was a social worker friend who had roped me into making my first national TV appearance. She had been a TV expert for years. Yet, when we were out to dinner and parties together, nobody recognized her, while they did recognize. What magic did I possess? I concluded it was my rapport with my audiences. Rapport buys us recognition and respect.

The harmony of rapport is at the base of every successful business exchange. Entrepreneurs who emphasize accomplishing a task over the importance of the people who perform it quickly derail. Audiences need to feel you acknowledge and appreciate them. Everyone wants to feel special. Everyone wants to feel the bond of a distinctive connection, a unique relationship with trusted rapport.

Quality relationships take time to evolve. Not only does every activity take longer than we generally expect, one researcher discovered that it actually takes 2.71828 times longer! Not many salespeople can brag about making a deal through one easy phone call. The seller must work on getting to know and understand each client.

Although a client may not be in a particular hurry for a connection to unfold, the salesperson must learn the choreography to the dance of patience. That means, she must defer gratification and accept rapport in small, incremental doses. This is a unique departure from the immediate gratification the rest of the world seeks.

3 Sequential Steps to Building Rapport

1. <u>Exchange non-personal pleasantries</u>:
    "How's the weather in St. Paul today?"
    "Who in our company was affected by the earthquake in Japan?"

2. <u>Pool common interests</u>
    "I wonder: did you attend New York University when I did?"
    "Doesn't our organization generate too much paperwork?"

3. <u>Open channels for further communications</u>
    "Would you like to join us for dinner tonight?"
    "If you decide to attend that concert, would you mind if I join you?"

These 3 sequential steps should take not more than a few minutes. Before a TV appearance with an anchor he had never met, Roger began an exchange with the usual, "Traffic was surprisingly light for a Monday morning." Small talk followed regarding the daily traffic in the area. Short on time before the interview was to begin on air, Roger continued with Step #2, "You graduated from Penn State. So did I." More quick small talk followed.

With a producer counting down their minutes to go live, Roger said, "Thank you for inviting me on today." And the show began with positivity and rapport as though the two had known each other for years. When such rapport is evident, the viewer picks up the positive vibes, and feels charmed and impressed by you. You can't lose. The last step, to open channels for further connection now becomes quick and easy. The interviewer will remember you, and you'll be invited back.

Applying the Rapport-Building Model

The Situation
John is attending a prestigious dinner. At a table across the room he spots the marketing manager of the firm he has been calling for the last 3 months. He has never been able to get through to this manager because the manager never returned any of his calls.

The Solution
This could be a challenging interchange. The marketing manager does not know John and his firm. But John assumes that the manager has received at least one of the many messages John left him.

Following the first 3 sequential steps, John approaches the manager, extends his hand, introduces himself, names his position and company, and says that he has been trying to reach him. John must be careful not to ask the manager why he never responded.

John exchanges a nonpersonal pleasantry (Step #1), such as, "How did your company get the idea for this event?"

After John gets his reply, he pools their common interests (Step #2) with, "I had heard your name mentioned often by Ray Smith, the person in charge of this affair. Did he coordinate the event with you? The manager describes how he knows Ray, and how they coordinated their efforts.

To open channels for further communications (Step #3), John asks, "I know people in my company who would support your cause. Are you planning another event like this one?"

Note the subject of discussion is neither John himself nor the manager, but rather the *situation*. Also note that out of the 3 possible approaches dealing with the situation, the *question* technique invites further communication. Finally, note that rather than asking questions that would result in brief, yes/no responses, John gets the manager to communicate with him in detail.

This interaction occurs without John mentioning what he can do for the marketing manager. There is no selling, but plenty of sharing and telling. Their exchange of words is preceded by EYE-ALOGUE and DYA-LOGUE. This rapport-building is the foundation of whatever is to follow. It takes just a few minutes.

If John senses positivity, he can organically move into a MONO-LOGUE about his product. He will now have a good chance of being received, not as a huckster who doesn't warrant a return call, but as a pleasant person with information or a product or a service that may be useful to the marketing manager.

The rewards of building rapport are great, especially in our relationship-oriented world. But building rapport is often misconstrued as "networking."

Networking Caution

During the height of an economic slowdown, I was receiving numerous phone calls from people I had not spoken to in years. Each of them began with, "I'm calling to do some networking with you." And then, "Do you know of any jobs in my field?"

Don't fall into that trap. Asking for favors is NOT networking. Networking is a result of *already-built* rapport during a time that there is no need. That takes time. It involves giving as well as taking. Just because you don't need something from a person during some period does not mean that you should not be visible to him or her. Send that person periodic articles that might be of interest to his job or industry. If this person's company is embattled in some controversy, offer your help. Ask to meet in person or virtually just to catch up.

A large company had contracted me to media train their executives. I had to fly to the company's headquarters. While sitting on the plane, I was writing an article about EYE-ALOGUE. The man sitting beside me chose to spy on what I was writing.

At first, I thought he was rude to be reading my private work. And then he was even bold enough to ask what EYE-ALOGUE was!! No shame there!! Instead of taking offense, however, we began to chat. I learned that he was the president of a diaper manufacturing company. As the flight continued, we discussed our personal lives, our business lives, and travel. When we landed, we exchanged business cards and that was the end—or so I thought.

The next week in the Wall Street Journal, I spotted an article about, of all things, diaper manufacturers. Before meeting this man, I never thought about this industry, because I was past the baby diaper stage and I was not nearing the adult diaper stage. Figuring this worldly man had probably read the article, I debated whether to send it to him. Then I reconsidered. We're all bombarded with information overload, so there might have been a chance this guy had missed reading it. So, I sent it.

A few days later, the man called to thank me. We agreed to stay in touch. I put him on my mailing list to receive articles I publish. And so it was for 5 years, sending, exchanging, thanking—with no ulterior motive in mind. Then one day, I received a call from the sales manager of this man's company. She recounted how 5 years earlier, the president and I had met on a plane. Now she was calling to ask if I would be the keynote speaker of their international sales conference!

I was shocked. I didn't know that this man's company was a large, international conglomerate. Diapers was such a foreign industry to me, I hadn't even thought to research this man's company, especially since I figured we'd never see each other again.

Of course, after the call from the sales manager, I did the needed exploration. And two months later, I was flying first class to a breathtaking Swiss ski chalet in Montreal, addressing international diaper executives!

The moral of this story is to be part of someone's network *when you don't need him for anything.* Let your rapport deepen. If you do need a favor in the future, you'll feel comfortable to ask and your contact will be willing to help. That's the height of "networking," or, more appropriately, "rapport."

Here's one way *not* to establish rapport. Susan and I met at a professional meeting. Very quickly, she called me her "good friend." I didn't care which appellation she used for our association because she seemed like a hard-working lady devoted to similar causes to mine (the Like Likes Like Dynamic). We were in touch sporadically, and that was fine.

Suddenly, she began calling me almost every early morning. Sometimes I wasn't available, and other times we spoke. She was seeking new employment and I listened to her job-hunting woes. She told a mutual friend that she called me often just to make sure I was okay. *We were never that close for her to be checking up on me, so I knew she was trying to impress our mutual friend.*

This woman's calls to me were totally about her, never asking how or what I was actually doing. Our mutual friend said she did the same with her—and she dropped their communication. A one-way network is no network at all. Eventually, our "good friend" status ended, just as it did with her and our mutual friend. If you want to network, be sure you incorporate the WIIFM? (What's In It For Me?). If your listener doesn't get a payoff from your interaction, the relationship will dissolve.

When was the last time you met someone you never thought would influence your life and career—only to learn you were wrong? Did you maintain contact with that person?

What did you learn from that experience?

As I say throughout this program, your media image impacts your income and promotions. Your income and promotions are built on strong relationships. Your relationships are formed because of your rapport. Your rapport evolves from continued interaction when you don't need it. Isn't it amazing how much begins and ends with how you project yourself?

Of course, you can't project what you aren't. And you can't project what you don't have. Oh, you might try, but the camera never lies. "Real" is what resonates with audiences. So, be your most real self, even occasionally when your audience sees you stumble. Laugh off your faux pas! As long as you're giving listeners their "What's In It For Me?," they'll believe that spending time with you has added value to them — and that's what everyone wants.

Whether you're on traditional or social media, it should never be about you, although it may seem that way. Actually, it's about YOUR AUDIENCE and the RAPPORT you build with them!! Start with strong 5-second soundbites. If you're effective you'll know it, because your listeners will want to expand those 5 seconds to much more time with you. Enjoy it, because it truly is fun seeing your audience derive so much from what you're giving them.

AMPLIFIER 57

CASE STUDY: BRAND STRATEGY OF A POLITICIAN WHO LOST

Arizona State Senator Martha McSally

In the southwest state of Arizona, after Senator John McCain died, Governor Doug Ducey filled McCain's vacant seat with Martha McSally, after her own loss to Senator Kyrsten Sinema. As two female candidates running against each other, McSally and Sinema had very different brand appearances and styles. Openly bisexual Sinema was always perfectly made up and coiffed. She looked and dressed like a sweet and trusted girl next door. But she also boasted educational credentials of a B.A., M.S.W., J.D., Ph.D., and M.B.A.

In contrast, Retired Air Force colonel, McSally became the first woman in U.S. history to fly a fighter jet in combat and to command a fighter squadron in combat. Usually without makeup with straight brown hair in a shoulder-length bob, she looked and dressed like an indistinguishable Plain Jane. The problem with being in media politics today is that your brand must stand out. She was an available and personable woman, but available and personable often doesn't win votes. Voters chose Sinema.

As politics would have it, McSally got a second chance. This time, she was in another race in Arizona in a special election for McCain's final two-year term. Her opponent was now

Democrat challenger, Mark Kelly, a former NASA astronaut, retired U.S. Navy captain, and husband of former U.S. Representative Gabrielle Giffords, who had been shot in the head and was never the same. The winner of this race would have to run again in 2022 for a full six-year term.

Kelly's war chest was an extraordinary $83 million, while McSally's was $52 million. He spent his money on bulleting her with relentless negative ads. McSally said they were lies, but she appeared as non-combative against her opposition's abundant negativity.

I met McSally's camp late in the race, with only a few weeks left for voters to cast their ballots. At that point, I knew any recommendations I had would merely be an academic exercise. Some on her team pushed for her to get a style change into starched white shirts and riding boots. I disagreed. It wasn't just the way she dressed; much more than that was needed.

McSally was usually in bland fitted dresses that looked well on her small frame. Who knew if she would even be comfortable discarding her usual clothing and changing to two-piece ensembles without the accompanying media coaching? It is for this reason that media coaching for a political candidate must be continuous over the course of many, many months, or even years.

For the most part, I thought the shirts vs. pants vs. skirts vs. dresses controversy was not that important, as long as her clothes were well-designed and attractive. Her shirt collars could have an open button or two to femininely and covertly signify she's not "buttoned-up." But these were mere superficial trimmings. And, again, would she be comfortable wearing them? If she were not, it would quickly show in her delivery of information.

More important than her clothing, I felt McSally needed work on how she carried herself, because this tiny fireball really didn't communicate an assertive enough stance for a United States Senator. Her hanging brown hair style could be layered and made more trendy. But she'd have to feel comfortable in this or any new look. Style change alone was not enough without the wherewithal to carry it off.

I believed her handlers were missing something vital. Since she had been a combat fighter, and since Kelly had launched such a nasty, angry race against her, maybe because he perceived her as a pushover female, I toyed with the idea of her donning COMBAT BOOTS! This choice could have been a pleasant change for her, because wearing high heels all day was not her preference. I boldly entertained COMBAT BOOTS as her new insignia, her brand. My idea was that this brand would be memorable, while quietly screaming, "I'm a tough fighter for YOU, my constituents!"

The woman had become the first female combat fighter in U.S. history, so combat boots would have gone well with her branding! Earlier, the voters had proved that she could not compete against the well-attired sweet girl image of a Kyrsten Sinema type. While McSally was petite, she was a strong woman whose strength was just not coming through. Of course, this situation was not helped by her need to responsibly wear a pandemic face mask while meeting and greeting people. For this, she needed a coach to show her how to use her eyes above that mask as piercing political artillery!

Rather than *defend* herself against Kelly's disgusting mud-slinging, she also needed to launch an OFFENSE. I spoke to her. I wondered if she would have been able to pull off a new Power Image if there had been time. I have worked with some who couldn't or wouldn't at first, and then adapted and shone as months went on.

I felt this politician would have benefited from training and re-packaging, but there were only weeks left before the final ballots were cast. These were merely my own musings. I knew that If anyone suddenly tries to hoist a new identity onto a candidate in the last moments of his or her campaign, it would only confuse voters and backfire.

The campaign did create an impressive print ad titled, "Less Flash, More Fight" with a photo of McSally in uniform, leaving a plane. The copy read, "I've been a fighter my whole life because I had to be. I lost my dad at age 12, I became a sexual abuse survivor at 17, and when I was told 'girls can't be fighter pilots,' I became the first female fighter pilot in combat. So when I tell you I will fight for Arizona in the Senate, it's coming from someone who's never backed down, and like our country, never encountered a challenge that couldn't be overcome. You want flashy, you've got a guy. If you want a fighter, I'm your girl."

The problem was that in her campaigning street garb, she looked exactly like a "girl," not the combat pilot that was part of her legacy.

On November 13, 2020, 10 days after polls closed, McSally conceded to her challenger, Mark Kelly, in her bid for the U.S. Senate. This ended the most expensive race in Arizona state history. We will never know what the outcome would have been had the McSally team employed different re-branding strategies.

AMPLIFIER 58

PART 9--FINALE
Humor Can Enhance Content

The first AMPLIFIER of PART 7 of this program began with, "Will Your Soundbites Keep Your Audience Awake?" I had been called upon to discuss the history of the New Year's Eve kiss. On face value, this could have turned into a pretty dull list of historical facts, so I was challenged. I decided to spice things up with a surprise statistic, offered in a surprising way, as you'll see in this video:
https://www.youtube.com/watch?v=pGgKADy2rbs

I introduced the humorous "kisslessness" fact to warm up the interviewers and the audience. Note that I slowed down my word delivery and pacing as I introduced the serious bacterial information. The male interviewer was surely taken aback, and laughed, "This took a turn to the south all of a sudden." That's when I knew I had hit the ball out of the park.

To fine tune your message, play with your concepts, frolic with your facts, and deliver them with surprise when you can. The more you keep your audience suspended in surprise, the more successful your interview will be. Everyone on set had a terrific time, and judging from my social media, so did our viewers.

1. This interview ran for almost 5 minutes. Did it keep you engaged? Why or why not?

2. What will you remember about this segment?

3. What would you have liked to see me change?

4. What would you do differently if you were on screen?

PART 10
GETTING APPLAUSE

DR. GILDA CARLE

AMPLIFIER 59

CASE STUDY: BRAND STRATEGY OF A POLITICIAN WHO WON

Arizona State Congresswoman Debbie Lesko

I met Debbie Lesko at a private event at a home in a posh community of Arizona. This politician had already been a congresswoman for two two-year terms, and there were only a few weeks left before the votes would be cast. My contacts told me she was a shoo-in, with a fairly easy re-election. She appeared to be a lovely, non-pretentious lady.

In contrast to the other pleasant, accessible politicians I met in Arizona, my own media indoctrination was in the snake pits of New York media and the crime-infested South Bronx streets. In those locations, political candidates were not lovely and non-pretentious. The Arizona crowd was very different. Although Lesko was assumed to be easily electable, I know there are no political definites, especially in the 2020 climate of cutthroat ruthlessness.

I studied this congresswoman's one local political debate on PBS Arizona with her political opponent, Michael Muscato. He was a 45-year old former baseball draft for the New York Yankees for a few seasons and now a gym owner. As I scrutinized the interaction, I noted that Muscato had a tough edge about him, but compared to New York politics where I had coached many combatants, he seemed mild:

https://www.pbs.org/video/10-05-20-debate-between-debbie-lesko-vs-michael-muscato-30aeoi/

With Wisconsin roots and a drawl-like speech pattern, 62-year-old Lesko opened the debate with her history of having been an abused wife and eventually a single mother. She remarked during the hour-long interaction how far she had come from those 35 abusive years earlier. I noted that she occasionally asked the male moderators for permission to speak (suggesting a submissive female). She also darted her eyes to the moderators after she made her statements (an approval-seeking move of timidity and tentativeness). When she said, "Excuse me, please," she giggled (which weakened her projection).

Donning my Relationship Expert hat, I quietly shook my head. I perceived this woman's scars of abuse. She seemed to still display wobbly equilibrium around men she deemed dominant. Had she been my client, I would have helped her overcome and outperform the evidence of these scars, especially on an all-eyes-on debate stage.

Lesko's strongest moments of the debate occurred during a powerful confrontation with her opponent. But it was halfway into her smiley discussion. Typically, that's when viewers are already gone, or, at least, they would already have made up their voting minds. So by then, her strong stance would likely have been lost to many.

In contrast, her opponent skillfully looked into the camera and addressed the voters with well-rehearsed sound bites and pre-crafted buzz phrases, like "guardianship over partisanship," "choose country over party," "We don't have a money problem; we have an appropriations problem," and "I'm one of yours, not a career politician." His media training was obvious—while Lesko clearly had none.

But then, Muscato began to lose momentum. In discussing the pandemic, he *whined* that he "lost his professional career and had his business shut down for 4 of the 6 months of the pandemic." Voters might have appreciated hearing how he used his leadership skills to find a solution to this fiscal dilemma. But he did not explain.

Wearing a black shirt and black tie, Muscato looked like a character from The Godfather. However, with his sartorial intimidation, he might have strongly introduced his ideas that could alter American history — and they might have been accepted. In doing further research, I found that while he boasted that he "travels all over the world" managing music groups, his timeline didn't jive with his "Yankees" story, running his gym business, and raising his family.

If Muscato had outlined his own fiscal success story to prove he could solve the problems of the nation, perhaps he would have had a chance. Instead, he complained that he was too poor to afford Obama health insurance and needed to find private insurance elsewhere.

Muscato's obvious media training was not enough. He hadn't connected and communicated how "being one of yours" empowered him to change the status quo. Connecting the dots is where many campaigns fall short. He never described what he would do differently from what Lesko had already done. Had I been his media coach, we would have rehearsed an outline of the problems of the country along with his solutions to right the wrongs. And there would not have been any confusion between the two.

Instead, he jabbed Lesko for voting against the Families First Coronavirus Response Act. She weakly defended (another note of timidity), "I didn't have time to read the bill." He angrily and nastily retorted that she had time to dance and fist-bump at some event. She responded that Nancy Pelosi gave Congress the Families First bill around 12:00 AM, with instructions to vote on it by 12:30. Nobody, including her, stood up against Pelosi for this unreasonable demand.

Lesko needed to display a greater force, so her opponent wouldn't even try to raise his maligning criticism. Muscato evidently sized her up as too nice — and her persona didn't negate his assessment.

Far into this debate, Lesko did name the three coronavirus aid bills she voted for. That comeback was substantial and direct, but again, it came too late in the program. Unlike the Godfather doppelgänger, she projected an air of down-home honesty and availability, telling her audience that she publishes her home number on her website, as she called for prayers and blessings for our country. That seemed to play well for her.

But politics can be dirty. A few days before the election, Lesko was thrown a curve ball with this critical article: **https://www.azcentral.com/story/opinion/op-ed/laurieroberts/2020/10/26/rep-debbie-lesko-kept-secrets-voters-had-right-know/6046410002/**

The writer was from the opposing aisle, and she accepted that Lesko was an abused wife, but now asked why she never explained the four aliases she had taken on, or her bankruptcies, or her arrest warrant, which eventually became a dismissed criminal charge. She even accused Lesko of profiting off her status as a victim of domestic violence.

The end of this article was especially weak: "Never having been a victim of domestic violence, it's difficult to understand why she didn't leave during the two and a half years this creeper was in prison the first time . . . "

If this writer had done her homework, she would have learned that it is common for victims of domestic violence to *not* leave their abusers because of what these monsters threaten. Such victims are brainwashed, they fear life in general—and that's why they coupled with their abuser in the first place—and their abusive mates are all they know.

Lesko's marriage to a con-artist who threatened to kill her and her daughter if they left him should have been enough for the writer to hear. What would anyone in an abusive marriage have done? We know what many women do: they stay longer than they should—and it's very dangerous. What would this accusing writer have done?

The Lesko campaign felt they needed to do damage control, a time-consuming effort while time was running short, and one that would only read as defensiveness. I counsel my media clients with *offense*, not defense. The campaign might have interviewed a psychologist or relationship expert on their website to explain what happens to people living under a roof of domestic terror. An aggressive public relations strategy could have been to position a local abuse expert on some of the television and radio networks, just to explain the syndrome. The writer, a female and mom herself, should have been more responsible.

Despite the negative press and her angry opponent, Debbie Lesko went on to win another two-year term in Arizona's 2020 8th Congressional District. However, as political races and federal interactions become more combative, if she intends to remain in the public eye, she will need to shed her girl-next-door niceness and strengthen her projection. Niceness is still interpreted as weakness, especially by bullies during contentious times. Lesko still needs to develop a tough skin so she's not mistaken for an easy mark by governmental tyrants, similar to what my client Dr. Jo Ivey Boufford had encountered in New York (See Amplifier 45).

AMPLIFIER 60

30-SECOND SOCIAL MEDIA COMMERCIAL

Now is your chance to apply your new media skills. Use a timer. In 30 seconds, the length of most commercials, on any social media portal, immediately hook our attention by promoting yourself. Not easy, is it? Outline your talking points first using the Speech Outline format in this program. Your objective is to be *remembered* and *referred*. Have someone assess your impact, or assess yourself when you view the playback.

1. How did you feel about the way this commercial looked?

2. Was 30 seconds enough time? Too much time?

3. How did it feel to promote yourself? What was comfortable and uncomfortable?

4. If you were part of the audience, would you remember and refer yourself?

5. As a result of this exercise, what will you do next?

AMPLIFIER 61

60-SECOND SOCIAL MEDIA COMMERCIAL

Now is your chance to apply your new media skills. Use a timer. In 60 seconds, on any social media portal, immediately hook audience attention by promoting yourself. People who haven't done this before say they feel awkward. Outline your talking points first using the Speech Outline in this course. Your objective is to be *remembered* and *referred*. Have someone assess your impact, or assess yourself when you view the playback.

1. How did you feel about the way this commercial looked?

2. Was 60 seconds enough time? Too much time? Easier for you than 30 seconds? Why?

3. How did it feel promoting yourself? What was comfortable and uncomfortable?

4. If you were part of the audience, would you remember and refer yourself?

5. As a result of this exercise, what will you do next?

AMPLIFIER 62

3-MINUTE MEDIA INTERVIEW

For this exercise, you will need a partner to play interviewer. You will also need a timer for 3 minutes. Pick the topic you want to discuss. Prepare 5 questions—and answers—you think an interviewer would ask about your topic. This interview could be live or virtual. It's your chance to showcase your expertise.

Hand your 5 prepared questions to your interviewer. (Sometimes, small media outlets do ask you to prepare questions for a show's host.) Projecting your best body posture, voice, and words, let your smarts and radiance shine!

1. Obviously, 3 minutes is much longer than 30 seconds or 60 seconds. If you're not thoroughly prepared, you can be taken off guard. Don't forget, there will be banter back and forth between you and the interviewer, perhaps laughter, perhaps questions off the topic. Yet, you only have 3 minutes. How do you feel you performed?

2. Was 3 minutes too long? Not long enough?

3. How would you compare the 30 second commercial, the 60 second commercial, and the 3-minute interview in terms of your ability to get your points across?

4. How did you like conversing with someone while you were supposed to be promoting yourself? Was it easier or more difficult?

5. Watch the playback. If you were in the audience, would you remember and refer yourself?

6. What did you learn from this experience?

DR. GILDA CARLE

AMPLIFIER 63

PART 10--FINALE
Respect Your Audience's Time

You've watched some of my TV interviews on different formats with different interviewers. You can go to my YouTube channel to see more (**https://youtube.com/c/drgilda**).

I intentionally wear solid bold colors or large patterns. Cameras seem to mute out pastels and white clothes. Also, little prints and patterns can "bleed" on the screen, making the viewers' eyes bleary.

I'm not always pleased with how what I'm wearing translates onto the screen. And we never know this in advance. So, it's not unusual for me to donate clothes that may feel right *before* an interview, but that turn out not to be flattering when I see the televised playback.

We are all works in progress. On the major networks, hosts have stylists to help them look great. When I taped the Dr. Gilda TV show pilot, Twentieth Century Fox provided a stylist who gave me clothing in which I felt stiff. Of course, that translated onto my performance. The best stylists know their clients and their comfort zones. But it's also up to us to voice our discomfort when clothes don't feel right for us.

The producer of a commercial I was taping sent me a run-down of clothes and jewelry I should and should not wear for our upcoming taping. Having been in this business for some time, I know what works on camera. On the day of the shoot, I chose to wear long, glittery earrings that televised beautifully on previous shows on which I had appeared.

The producer was not happy when she saw them on me. I respectfully told her that I'd worn them before, and the camera loves them. Disbelieving, she remained unhappy about this.

The shoot went magnificently. The producer apologized and said she was shocked how well the earrings looked. Not all "professionals" know what they're talking about. Go with your gut and your experience. When you're empowered on camera, the audience feels it. Cameras never lie!

Watch this: "What Is an It-Girl?":
https://www.youtube.com/watch?v=K2NoKhxu4ZQ&t=60s

This clip is only 2 minutes, 2 seconds long. After seeing this video, schools and colleges have hired me to speak and offer my relationship advice. **Getting hired is tantamount to applause!**

1. Did this brief interview keep you engaged? Why or why not?

2. What will you remember about this segment?

3. What would you have liked to see me change?

4. What would you do differently if you were on screen?

DR. GILDA CARLE

AMPLIFIER 64

END NOTES

Every major player on TV and radio has had Media Coaching. Let's review your skill set now.

1. My media strengths are:

2. The skills I must master better are:

3. I know I'm being too hard on myself when:

    If being hard on yourself is your issue, study these words:

    <u>Gilda-Gram®</u>:
    **You will never be loved
    if you don't risk being disliked.**

4. Are you willing to risk being disliked in a public arena? Whenever you step out, there will be people who disagree. But if you don't go beyond your protective bubble, people who need your expertise won't know about it or you. You may think that public projection puts you on the line. But remember, you're merely the vehicle through which information is dispensed. If you don't risk being out there, your brand will never be loved.

Because employees' media presence affects a company's bottom line, companies often subsidize employees' professional coaching.

AMPLFIER 65

GILDA-GRAMS® IN THIS BOOK

<u>Gilda-Gram®</u>
Use the power you have,
or lose the power you had.

<u>Gilda-Gram®</u>
There are no failures,
only lessons in what to do next.

<u>Gilda-Gram®</u>
The shorter your time,
the more challenging your task.

<u>Gilda-Gram®</u>
If you want to succeed,
amplify your media presence.

<u>Gilda-Gram®</u>
Do something every day
that makes you feel uncomfortable.

<u>Gilda-Gram®</u>
No one pays attention without knowing
"What's In It For Me?"

<u>Gilda-Gram®</u>
Time spent with me
adds value to you.

<u>Gilda-Gram®</u>
What we learn,
we can also unlearn.

Gilda-Gram®
Like likes like.

Gilda-Gram®
All audiences want to sense
they are seen.

Gilda-Gram®
When in doubt, do without.

Gilda-Gram®
Emotions and Feelings
motivate buying and buying into.

Gilda-Gram®
True relatability replaces
the SELL with the TELL--
and adds FEELINGS.

Gilda-Gram®
The Taskmaster who feels out of control
aims to control others.

Gilda-Gram®
The Toastmaster who feels without control
becomes depressed and/or angry
for suppressing his own voice.

Gilda-Gram®
When you like yourself, you trust yourself.
When you trust yourself, you voice your feelings.

Gilda-Gram®
Power is never control *over*.
Over-control verifies a person's insecurity.

Gilda-Gram®
Power is as power does.
Power does as power feels.
Power feels as power thinks.
Think power, project power.

Gilda-Gram®
Content must be appealing,
and delivery must be compelling.

Gilda-Gram®
Your objective is to be
REMEMBERED and REFERRED.

Gilda-Gram®
Guide your seer to see you
exactly as you want to be seen.

Gilda-Gram®
When something happens TO us,
It really happens FOR us.

Gilda-Gram®
It's <u>5</u> seconds before an audience's
first mental vacation.

Gilda-Gram®
The way you present your goblet
determines how others will fill it.

Gilda-Gram®
You will never be loved
if you don't risk being disliked.

AMPLIFIER 66

MORE OF DR. GILDA'S COUNSEL

***

BUSINESS COACHING & PERSONAL ADVICE
Register at: www.DrGilda.com

***

BOOKS on AMAZON

Dr. Gilda's Relationship Series
--8 Steps to a Sizzling Marriage
--8 Tips to Understand the Opposite Sex
--10 Questions Single Women Should Never Ask & 10 They Should
--10 Signs of a Cheater-to-Be

Dr. Gilda's Self-Worth Series
--I'm Worth Loving! Here's Why.
--Ask for What You Want – AND GET IT!
--How to Be a Stress-Free, Worry-Free Woman

Dr. Gilda's Fidelity Series
--Your Cheater Keeps Cheating – And You're Still There
--How to Cope with the Cheater You Love
--99 Prescriptions for Fidelity: Your Rx for Trust

Business Book
--One-Up Strategies Business Schools Don't Teach

More Relationship Books
--Don't Bet on the Prince! How to Have the Man You Want by Betting on Yourself
--Don't Lie on Your Back for a Guy Who Doesn't Have Yours
--My Rants & Ramblings Journal (365 Gilda-Grams® for Every Day of the Year)

Media Coaching
--Amplify Your Media Presence, Amplify Your Brand

REACH DR. GILDA ON SOCIAL MEDIA

LinkedIn: https://**www.linkedin.com/in/drgilda**
Facebook: https://**www.facebook.com/drgilda**
Instagram: https://**www.instagram.com/drgilda**
Twitter: https://**www.twitter.com/drgilda**
YouTube: **https://youtube.com/c/drgilda**

Website: **https://www.drgilda.com**

CONCLUSION

This is just the beginning of your power projection. Keep reviewing these basics, keep rehearsing, and keep continuing to appear in front of everyone who requests you to speak. It's natural that some days you may not feel you're ready to shine. "Do It Anyway," as Martina McBride titled one of her country songs. The more you're out there, the more comfortable you'll feel.

As you watch each of your appearances, you will begin to sense an air of confidence that you did not have when you began. The media success equation is simple: The more comfortable and confident you feel, the more quickly your audiences will trust you. The more your audiences trust you, the more quickly they will clamor for your brand.

Don't fret, because you're never alone on your journey! Email me at **Staff@DrGilda.com** that you've read this book, and I will answer your quick questions at no cost. For greater depth, register for my private online coaching at **www.DrGilda.com**.

I want you to succeed. Please let me know how I can support that effort. Here's to projecting your unique Power Image!

Dr. Gilda

REFERENCES

INTRODUCTION

Grose, Pamela. (2021, January 13). "Is Remote Work Making Us Paranoid?" The New York Times.

Robert Half, PR Newswire. (2020, November 12). "Nearly 4 in 10 Workers Are Suffering from Video Call Fatigue. Robert Half Research Shows Technical Issues and Too Many Participants Are Biggest Virtual Meeting Pet Peeves.

"The State of Employee Engagement and Experience in 2020," www.Glintinc.com

Harter, Jim. (2020, July 2). "Historic Drop in Employee Engagement Follows Record Rise," Gallup.

Cameron, Doug and Morath, Eric. (2021, January 17). "Covid 19's Blow to Business Travel is Expected for Years," The Wall Street Journal.

Wallace, Brian. (2021, January 14) "Will Remote Work Create a Larger Wage Gap?" Thrive Global, www.thriveglobal.com.

Needham, Jack. (2021, January 2021). "No, Don't Smoke in Zoom Meetings," WIRED.

Amplifier 1

Coroy, Kat. Branding Expert, UK and Instagram. www.katcoroy.com

Balliett, Amy. Founder and CEO of Killer Visual Strategies, visual communication agency, Seattle, Washington.

Amplifier 4

Rogers, Kenny. (1978). Singer, *The Gambler*, song written by Don Schlitz in 1976.

Amplifier 9

Bartleby. (23 January 2021). "The Secrets of Successful Listening: Lessons from a Hostage Negotiator," The Economist. www.economist.com.

Amplifier 13

Godin, Seth. (2018). *This is Marketing: You Can't Be Seen Until You Learn to See.* Penguin Random House.

Pahwa, Aashish. Founder, Feedough.com, resource for startups. East Delhi, Delhi, India.

Ekman, Paul. (2009, Revised). *Telling Lies: Clues to Deceit in the Marketplace, Politics, and Marriage.* W. W. Norton & Company.

Killingsworth, Mathew A. and Gilbert, Daniel T. (2010, November 12). "A Wandering Mind Is an Unhappy Mind," Science Magazine, www.sciencemag.org

Amplifier 14

Billions" (2016 +). Showtime TV series about power politics in the world of New York high finance.

Amplifier 15

Cohen, Heidi. (2020, January 5, 2021). "AMG Newsletter [Actionable Marketing Guide]." www.HeidiCohen.com.

Amplifier 17

Carle, Dr. Gilda. (2011). *Don't Bet on the Prince! How to Have the Man You Want by Betting On Yourself.* InterChange Communications Training, Inc.

Amplifier 19

Eber, Karen. (February 2020). *How Your Brain Responds to Stories -- and Why They're Crucial for Leaders.* Tedx Perdue University. https://www.ted.com/talks/karen_eber_how_your_brain_responds_to_stories_and_why_they_re_crucial_for_leaders?utm_source=newsletter_daily&utm_campaign=daily&utm_medium=email&utm_content=image__2021-01-14

Amplifier 26

Leadem, Rose. (2018, August 12). "Why Emotional Intelligence Is Crucial for Success (Infographic); Having a High EQ is Just As Important as a High IQ," Entrepreneur.com.

Nguyen, Kelli. (2021, January 12). "Bosses Get a New Job Description," LinkedIn News.

Cumello, Joe. (2020, November 30). "How to Hire for Emotional Intelligence—A Practical Guide in the Age of Covid-19," Fast Company.

Brown, Lee. (2021, January 5). "Antwerp Mayor Caught Wearing Underwear during Livestreamed Interview," New York Post.

Amplifier 40

Carle, Dr. Gilda. (2011). *Don't Bet on the Prince! How to Have the Man You Want by Betting on Yourself.* InterChange Communications Training, Inc.

Crossing Delancey (1988). Warner Bros. Films.

Amplifier 44

Hall, Edward T. (1990). *The Hidden Dimension.* Anchor Books.

Hunt, Valeria V. (1995). *Infinite Mind: Science of the Human Vibrations of Consciousness.* Jenson Books Inc.

Satir, Virginia. (2009, Revised). *Your Many Faces: The First Step to Being Loved.* Celestial Arts

Buscaglia, Leo. (1996). *Love: What Life Is All About.* Ballantine Books.

Amplifier 46

Carle, Dr. Gilda. (2011). *Don't Bet on the Prince! How to Have the Man You Want by Betting on Yourself.* InterChange Communications Training, Inc.

Amplifier 47

Carle, Dr. Gilda. (1989, March). "Handling a Hostile

Audience--with Your Eyes," *IEEE, world's largest professional association for the advancement of technology.*

www.ingramcontent.com/pod-product-compliance
Lightning Source LLC
LaVergne TN
LVHW051114080426
835510LV00018B/2040